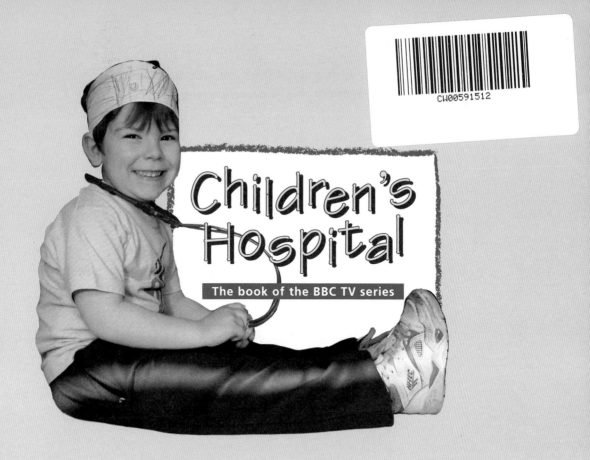

Children's Hospital

The book of the BBC TV series

BBC Books

For every copy of the book sold, money will be donated to Sheffield Children's Hospital.

The Authors

Children's Hospital

This book is published to accompany the television series entitled *Children's Hospital* which was first broadcast in the Autumn of 1993.

Designed and produced by Parke Sutton Publishing Limited, The Old Tannery, Barrack Street, Norwich NR3 1TS.

Published by BBC Books, a division of BBC Enterprises Limited, Woodlands, 80 Wood Lane, London W12 0TT.

First published 1993
Copyright © Richard Bradley, Tracy Cook, Lisa Perkins and Mark Phillips 1993
ISBN 0 563 36972 8

Edited by Anne Priestley
Designed by Kim Smith
Photographs by John Peters (except those listed below)

Additional photographs by David Bocking (pp. 12, 30, 32, 91); Richard Bradley (p.6); Alun Bull (p. 90); Martin Jenkinson (p. 126).
Typeset by PS Typesetting
Printed and bound in Great Britain by BPCC Paulton Books Ltd, Bristol
Colour separation by Hilo Offset Ltd, Colchester
Cover printed in Great Britain by Clays Ltd, St Ives plc

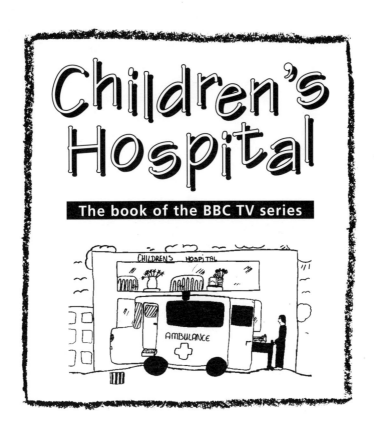

Children's Hospital

The book of the BBC TV series

Richard Bradley

Tracy Cook

Lisa Perkins

Mark Phillips

BBC Books

Acknowledgements

Having spent many months in the inspiring atmosphere of Sheffield Children's Hospital, the authors hope that this book will convey a sense of the very special place it is. We have been privileged to witness some of the best care our National Health Service provides, and we strongly echo the feelings expressed by one mother in this book that care of this kind should be a right for every child and not a matter of geographical chance.

In compiling a book like this, we make demands on the time and patience of many, but can use the contributions of only a few. Though we are able to reflect just a fraction of the work undertaken in the hospital, we should like to extend our warmest thanks to *all* those who work there, and particularly those whose effort we were not able to include. There is so much good work taking place in every corner of the hospital, we would need a book many times the size of this one to do it justice.

Fortunately, very few children have to spend as long at SCH as we have, though it has been anything but an endurance test. Everyone has put up with us with patience and good humour, and we have received wonderful co-operation, even when attempting to cram a crew and camera gear into the smallest of cubicles.

Several of the contributions in this book have come from staff who have given their time after hours to write or be interviewed by us. The nursery nurses deserve special thanks for inspiring the children to create the pieces in this book.

We should also like to thank all the parents who allowed us to be with them at the most stressful and emotional of times. Their trust and openness was crucial to the success of the project.

Thanks are also due to Tracy, who had the idea in the first place, and to those behind the scenes in production. A special thankyou to Alex Harris for cheerful support while typing the manuscript; to photographer John Peters and to the film editors, Margaret Kelly and Tony Heaven, who worked so hard to give the series shape; to the camera crew who we dragged away from their own children for so much of the year, especially to Martin Lightening, Chris Atkinson, Mike James and Chris Sugden-Smith. Back at base, Steve Hewlett and Bhupinder Kohli kept us on track.

We owe thanks also to Peter Harvey, the historian of the Children's Hospital, and to Mothercare for the Accident Prevention advice.

But of course it is the children of Sheffield and beyond whom we have most to thank – for the many pictures and pieces they have contributed, for allowing us to film with them, and for making the whole process so much fun. Without them there would have been no TV series and no book.

RICHARD BRADLEY   LISA PERKINS

TRACY COOK   MARK PHILLIPS

Foreword

Hello I'm Chris Waddle. There are many good things about Sheffield. Two of the best are the team I play for – Sheffield Wednesday – and the Children's Hospital! So I'm delighted to have the chance to write the Foreword for this book about the hospital.

Here at Hillsborough we are proud of our close links with the hospital. Team players often go up there to meet the children, and have been involved in raising money. Ossie Owl is a frequent visitor to the wards. We hope we play a small part in helping children get through their time in hospital. I know we value the support we've had from the children and staff all season.

As a team we pride ourselves on dedication and professionalism. The staff at the hospital show those qualities in great abundance. I'd like to offer my support to the hospital as it continues to look after our children – and who knows, some future Wednesday players.

It's been a good season for us – I'd like to wish the Children's Hospital well too. I hope you all enjoy this book.

Sheffield Wednesday
Football Club PLC

CHRIS WADDLE

Sheffield Children's Hospital

Introduction

The Sheffield Children's Hospital is delighted to be associated with BBC Television in the production of this book. In its pages you will find an account of some of the children who have been treated in our hospital and of the staff, nurses, doctors, therapists, technicians and many others who make up the team of carers in a modern hospital. We were perhaps surprised but certainly pleased to be chosen as the hospital in which a TV series was to be made; our only request was that no child or parent would appear in the final programme without his or her permission. I am sure that some of our patients and staff will emerge as TV characters, the sort of people who add a sense of heightened realism to a recording of our everyday life; we need their input to understand the mixture of success and sometimes sadness that makes up our working day.

The hospital was founded in 1876 in what was, even then, an old house on the outskirts of Sheffield, when a family doctor, Dr Cleaver, raised money for six cots to be provided and staffed. By 1888 more room was needed, and two houses were bought on the site of our present hospital. Two purpose-built wards were added and in 1903 our red-brick corner building was opened, the beginning of a quarter-mile frontage up Western Bank. Further building followed, and our newest block was opened by the Princess of Wales in 1989.

While the original hospital looked after Sheffield children from poor families, we now provide a specialised in-patient and out-patient service for any child in the north part of the Trent Region, including Barnsley, Rotherham, Doncaster, Worksop and Chesterfield. In addition, we admit children from all over Britain for specialised treatment, such as leg-lengthening, and some from overseas, including those from war- and famine-stricken areas.

By the 1970s we had grown to a size of about 250 beds overall. However, now with about 130 beds we can treat many more children due to shorter average stays in hospital, about three to four days at present. Some surgery is now 'day case' with discharge on the same day as admission. We all believe that, as long as parents can cope, children are better if simple treatment can be given at home.

We have recently become a Trust hospital within the NHS; this will preserve our identity and so continue the specialism and quality of our work.

Finally, I should like to thank the BBC team for the sensitive way in which they have worked with hospital staff, capturing the humour as well as the drama of everyday activities without disturbing the pattern of patient care. I hope that the TV series and this book will be a source of interest and encouragement to families, staff and our many supporters alike.

DR KEITH LEVICK
Chief Executive
Sheffield Children's Hospital NHS Trust

What's Special about a Children's Hospital

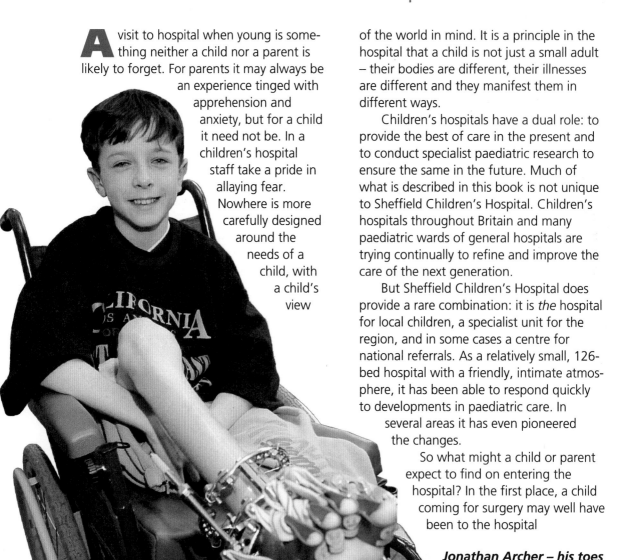

A visit to hospital when young is something neither a child nor a parent is likely to forget. For parents it may always be an experience tinged with apprehension and anxiety, but for a child it need not be. In a children's hospital staff take a pride in allaying fear. Nowhere is more carefully designed around the needs of a child, with a child's view of the world in mind. It is a principle in the hospital that a child is not just a small adult – their bodies are different, their illnesses are different and they manifest them in different ways.

Children's hospitals have a dual role: to provide the best of care in the present and to conduct specialist paediatric research to ensure the same in the future. Much of what is described in this book is not unique to Sheffield Children's Hospital. Children's hospitals throughout Britain and many paediatric wards of general hospitals are trying continually to refine and improve the care of the next generation.

But Sheffield Children's Hospital does provide a rare combination: it is *the* hospital for local children, a specialist unit for the region, and in some cases a centre for national referrals. As a relatively small, 126-bed hospital with a friendly, intimate atmosphere, it has been able to respond quickly to developments in paediatric care. In several areas it has even pioneered the changes.

So what might a child or parent expect to find on entering the hospital? In the first place, a child coming for surgery may well have been to the hospital

Jonathan Archer – his toes decorated with pictures of the hospital staff.

already: children are often invited to look around the wards sometime before an operation. Those due for major surgery, such as leg-lengthening, are even invited to spend a night in hospital to try it out. But for most, coming to hospital is a surprise – and a pleasant one.

No institutional green or magnolia walls here – all the wards and corridors are decorated with murals. The monitors on Intensive Care sit amid hand-painted clowns, clouds and cartoon characters. On the doors of the operating theatres at a child's height are more colourful paintings. And, to stop a child straying too far, all the door handles in the hospital are at adult height.

On admission a child is escorted to the ward, and introduced to the others in the bay. You might overhear a nurse asking a baby's parents, 'Does she have a teddy?' and, 'What is teddy's name?' It is all part of striking up a rapport with the child. Each child has a named nurse assigned to them, and the name of each nurse is on a colourful badge pinned to his or her uniform. There is not a white coat to be seen – the doctors abandoned them several years ago.

Each ward boasts a nursery nurse with toys for all ages, and a library of videos and computer games keeps older boys and girls occupied. Bored siblings can be left in the Roof House, a great supervised playroom perched on the hospital roof. Next door are rooms for mums and dads to stay overnight: some wards even allow parents to unfold a Z-bed and settle down next to the patient. Visiting hours disappeared over a decade ago. Parents and relatives are encouraged

The Good Old Days?

Attitudes to child care have changed beyond recognition from those preached earlier this century. Who today would defend John B. Watson, infant-care theorist writing in 1928?

'The sensible way to bring up children is to treat them as young adults. . . . Let your behaviour always be objective and kindly firm. Never hug and kiss them. Never let them sit in your lap. If you must, kiss them once on the forehead when they say goodnight. Shake hands with them in the morning. Give them a pat on the head if they have made an extremely good job of a difficult task. Try it out. In a week's time you will find out how easy it is to be perfectly objective with your child and at the same time kindly. You will be ashamed of the mawkish, sentimental way you have been handling it.'

Drawing by Sarah Cabry Age 9

to stay as long as they feel able.

As treatment begins the real differences between this and many hospitals emerge. A clear, illustrated guide with pictures is given to each child awaiting an operation. It contains photos of the people the children are likely to meet along the way. The emphasis is on simple explanation in words a child will understand. It also often answers questions a parent might be too embarrassed to ask. As a result many children are far better able to explain their illness and treatment than adults in the same situation.

Before an operation a child must make a visit to the phlebotomist for blood

samples. For adults this would mean a syringeful of blood each time. Since no child likes the sight of big needles, however, all the basic full blood counts are done from only half a millilitre of blood. This tiny amount can be collected from a thumb or heel prick.

As an operation nears many children get anxious. Here the nursery nurses come into their own with a variety of stress-relieving games to play: a little boy awaiting an ear operation is shown what to expect by bandaging his teddy's ears, a girl in the Orthopaedic Ward is shown a doll in a thigh-to-ankle plaster. The child dons a colourful, patterned operation gown rather than a traditional white one. Children on the Day Care Ward can even choose their means of transport to the Theatre – a battery-powered police motorbike, for instance – although many enjoy the treat of a ride on the more conventional trolley.

The trip to Theatre need not be on a trolley.

Before the anaesthetic, 'magic cream' is rubbed on the backs of each child's hands. Emla cream is a local anaesthetic, widely used throughout the hospital, which makes an injection painless. In the anaesthetic room itself a parent may be called into action to read a story to their child as he or she is given 'magic wind', or gas. Even the lead X-ray aprons needed for certain operations are brightly patterned.

Of course, these are only some of the external things a visitor would notice. Less immediately obvious but as important is having the back-up of staff specialised in paediatric care. They are staff with experience gained from treating thousands of children: nurses with Sick Children qualifications, anaesthetists used to tiny patients, a pathology lab skilled at interpreting small specimens from small people, paediatricians used to speaking to parents and children in terms both will understand, social workers who know how hard it is to juggle work, family and a sick child, porters used to ferrying anxious children to Theatre, and nursery nurses trained to minimise that anxiety.

It all seems so sensible, it is hard to imagine there was ever any objection to the principle of a specialist children's hospital. But there was such a time, and it was not long ago.

The Story of the Hospital

Two centuries ago there was not a single specialist children's hospital in Britain. No one seemed to think that they were a good idea. A 'Dispensary for the Infant Poor' was opened in 1796. But its founder, George Armstrong, had a string of objections to a children's hospital, and several of his concerns were shared by much more modern reformers: 'Such a scheme as this can never be executed. If you take away a sick child from its parent or nurse, you break its heart immediately.' If each child required a nurse, the hospital would become impossibly large. Putting children with adult nurses would contaminate the air, and nurses and mothers would continually argue over their children. The children in turn would keep each other awake with crying, and by 'vomiting and purging' pass on all their ailments to each other. Last but not least, he sharply observed, 'It very seldom happens that a mother can conveniently leave the rest of her family to go into an Hospital to attend to her sick infant.'

Across the Channel, such obstacles did not prevent the founding of the first special hospital for children in 1802, in Paris. The revolutionary idea was taken up all over Europe, and soon Berlin, Vienna, St Petersburg, Turin and even Constantinople had their own.

In Britain, however, influential opposition continued. Even Florence Nightingale believed children's hospitals to be a bad idea. If sick children had to come into hospital at all, she felt they were better placed on adult wards. A woman in the next bed would become 'the child's best protector and nurse. And it does her as much good as it does the child.' And anyway, Miss Nightingale asked, where would the nurses be found? 'There must be a real, genuine vocation and love for the work; a feeling as if your own happiness were bound up in each particular child's recovery. Nothing else will carry you through the perpetual wear and tear of the spirits, of the fretfulness, the unreasonableness, of sick children – not that I think it is greater than that of many sick adults – but it is more wearing, because the strain is never off a minute.' But the tide flowed against the Lady of the Lamp.

The first children's hospital appeal was launched by physician Charles West, who had run a 'Universal Dispensary for Children'. In 1852 the famous Hospital for Sick Children, Great Ormond Street, opened its doors to its first small patients. The London hospital was followed by others in Liverpool, Manchester and Edinburgh, and by 1888 there were 38 such hospitals in Britain: one of these was Sheffield Children's Hospital.

In 1876, the year the Children's Hospital opened in Sheffield, the town was not a healthy place. During the year, 3218 of the city's children (nearly one in five) died before their fifth birthday. At the heart of the Industrial Revolution, the town could not escape the ills that it brought in its wake. Each day, millions of gallons of solid and liquid filth poured into the Don and its

Nurse's Day

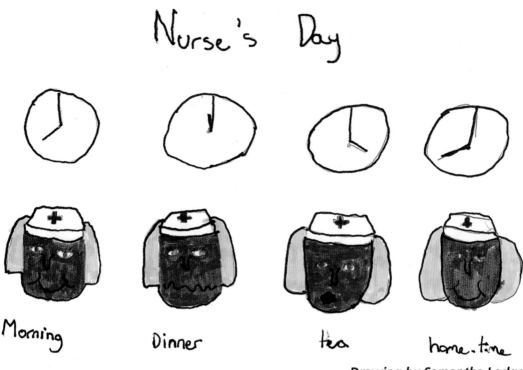

Morning   Dinner   tea   home.time

Drawing by Samantha Lodge

tributaries. In only 70 years, the population had increased fivefold as migrants abandoned the country in search of work in the mills and forges. Crumbling, cramped housing, sewage in the streets and streams, bad drainage and a poor water supply in private hands made life for many a misery.

For the children, it was a battle simply to survive – and many did not. Child labour was widespread, and so was injury at work. Few children saw doctors – they were too expensive.

In this grim climate a young doctor (28-year-old Dr William Cleaver), an architect and a solicitor, with a group of sympathisers, took a small but far-reaching step.

On 15 November 1876 the Sheffield Free Hospital for Sick Children opened at Brightmore House on Brookhill. At £65 a year they could only afford an old property which was 'not very eligible in sanitary respects'. Still, by the year's end, the first 45 patients had passed through.

Despite the death of its main founder, Dr Cleaver, from pneumonia in 1895, the hospital survived its growing pains. Now known as the Children's Hospital, it moved to a smarter home on Western Bank. Here the hospital flourished. As the new century began it was seeing 250 children as in-patients and 2000 more as out-patients each year.

A wealthy benefactor made possible the opening of an East End branch of the hospital which operated for 38 years and treated some 300 000 children.

Child Deaths in Sheffield, 1876

Without immunisation and vaccination, 3218 children under five years old in Sheffield died in 1876. These are some of the causes.

Smallpox	1
Measles	152
Scarlatina	184
Diphtheria	13
Croup	43
Whooping cough	130
Fevers, including typhus and enteric	58
Diarrhoea and dysentery	417
Cholera	3
Erysipelas (a skin infection)	6
Bronchitis, pneumonia and pleurisy	623
Injuries	5
Heart disease	3
Other causes	1580

(*from the report of the Medical Officer for Health, 1876*)

As the work of the hospital developed, it was joined in the battle against infant mortality by the city council. The first health visitors were appointed, drainage and rubbish collection was improved, old privies were turned into water closets. Medical inspections began in schools, and in 1907 needy children were provided with free school meals. By 1914, when the First World War broke out, 14 000 children a year were being treated at the Children's Hospital.

Always short of funds for an expanding service, a most successful scheme was launched in 1921. Known as the Penny in the £ scheme, Sheffield working people subscribed a penny a week for each pound they earned. Their employers added a third of the sum raised. In return, they received free treatment at any of Sheffield's voluntary hospitals. By the time the National

Health Service was launched in 1948, the scheme had raised nearly £5 million. It virtually doubled the hospital's income.

The late 1940s were important years for the hospital. In 1947 Sheffield University had opened a Department of Child Health at the hospital, headed until 1975 by the famous child health specialist Professor Ronald Illingworth. The Children's Hospital became a part of the newly formed NHS. And there was good news for all children who lived in fear of tuberculosis: the revolutionary drug streptomycin was first used at this time and, almost overnight, child deaths from TB plummeted.

The Cleaver Ward, which was built in memory of the hospital's founding doctor and opened in 1896.

Sheffield Children's Hospital in its Early Years

● Nurses' pay was £10 a year, and they were allowed twice-weekly breaks for recreation, and once on Sundays for church. But they worked over eleven hours a day, seven days a week.

● Children's families and friends could visit for just two hours a week – on Thursdays and Sundays from 3 p.m. to 4 p.m.

● Bringing food in for patients was strictly forbidden.

● For £20 a year a well-wisher could endow a cot and nominate a patient for it whenever it was free.

● Even in those early days, money was always a problem. Just two years after opening, the hospital could only use eight of its twelve beds because of a dire shortage of funds.

● An average of one new patient a day was seen in 1876, the Children's Hospital's first year.

SCH Admissions, 1992

In 1992 there were a total of 12 340 admissions to the Children's Hospital.

Dental surgery	142
Dermatology (skin conditions)	9
Ear, Nose and Throat (commonly grommets, tonsils, adenoids)	1228
Haematology (blood disorders like anaemia, leukaemia)	617
Oncology (childhood cancer)	245
Ophthalmology	1
Oral Surgery	99
Orthopaedics	1273
Paediatric Neurology (such as epilepsy, cerebral palsy, Down's)	174
Paediatric Surgery (commonly hernias, appendicectomies, undescended testes)	2960
Paediatrics (such as bronchitis, asthma, diabetes, tonsilitis febrile convulsions, ingestions)	4841
Plastic Surgery (such as birthmark removal, pinning back ears, burns)	673
Radiology	78

By the 1950s the Children's Hospital was beginning to emerge as today's visitors would recognise it. From 1952, daily visiting for half an hour was permitted. Teachers were brought in for the long-stay patients. A pathology department solely for children was opened. Pioneering research was carried out in rheumatic fever, hydrocephalus (water on the brain) and spina bifida.

Today over a century old, the hospital continues to see more children from further afield each year, yet at no stage in its life has the future of the Children's Hospital been secure. In April 1992 the hospital became a Trust, as senior staff believed this was the best way of ensuring its survival and independence. The hospital that began with a dozen beds and no running water now wrestles with the more complex problems of a health market-place: fighting for every penny it spends from health authorities, fund-holding GPs and extra-contractual referrals. It has to balance ever-tighter budgets with the pressure to treat ever more children. Meanwhile, the health authorities juggle the competing priorities of primary health care, the elderly, mental health, adults and children. In a rough sea, the hospital continues to stay afloat.

With a staff of 800, a budget of £20 million, 126 beds and three operating theatres, SCH is a small but busy hospital.

In the pages that follow, with the help of staff, parents and children, we guide you through this special world where adults work for children.

Hospital Who's Who

Care and treatment for a child in hospital has always been a team effort. But as care gets more sophisticated and specialised, the numbers grow. To a sick child or parent so many strange faces can seem bewildering. Below is a list of some of the people a child might meet in hospital, and several more who work behind the scenes on the children's behalf:

Medical student

Senior house officer (SHO)

Casualty officer

Registrar

Senior registrar

Consultant

Professor

Anaesthetist

Operating department assistant (ODA)

Operating department orderly (ODO)

Pathologist

Micro-biologist

Radiographer

Radiologist

Child psychologist

Ward clerk

Nursery nurse

Support worker

Student nurse

Enrolled nurse

Staff nurse

Sister/Charge nurse

Phlebotomist

Porter

Domestic

Social worker

Physiotherapist

Speech therapist

Occupational therapist

Dietitian

Pharmacist

Community nurse

Teacher

Chaplain

Drawing by Ella Besharati
Age 9

Here is a brief description of what some of these people do:

Medical student: a student doctor in the second half of their training, one to three years away from qualifying.

SHO or senior house officer: a junior doctor working on the wards or in theatre; qualified for at least a year.

Casualty officer: a different name for a doctor working in casualty.

Registrar/senior registrar: a more senior doctor in training, working on the wards, in theatre and in out-patient clinics. They supervise SHOs.

Consultant: the head of the team of doctors, ultimately responsible for all the patients under their care. Is either a physician who treats acute illnesses and chronic diseases, or a surgeon who operates. Physicians are known as Dr; surgeons as Mr or Miss. A consultant has a speciality or area of expertise. For example, neurology (the nervous system) or gastro-enterology (stomach and intestines). In the Children's Hospital most are specialist paediatricians as well, but some of the surgeons do operate on adults.

Professor: the post has the same status as that of consultant but is linked to a university. Professors have extra responsibilities for research and training.

Anaesthetist: a doctor who specialises in anaesthetics. Not just involved in putting children to sleep for operations, but also in the vital ventilation of children on intensive care and resuscitation.

ODA or operating department assistant: a technician who sets up and maintains all anaesthetic equipment, assists in anaesthesia and is part of the resuscitation team.

ODO or operating department orderly: a porter who ferries children between the operating theatres and the wards.

Pathologist: a highly-trained doctor who analyses specimens in the labs. A lot of the work involves the use of microscopes.

Micro-biologist: a specialist in growing and identifying bacteria.

Radiographer: a person trained in taking X-rays and scans.

Radiologist: a medically qualified doctor who reads or interprets X-rays and scans.

Child psychologist: trained to deal with behavioural or emotional problems; not a medical doctor.

Ward clerk: a clerical assistant on the wards who helps to organise notes, admissions and results.

Nursery nurse: a specialist in play, helping children pass the time and play out their fears and anxieties.

Support worker: a person who provides support and assistance to the nursing staff; may have a national vocational qualification.

Student nurse: all student nurses in Sheffield are part of Project 2000. They take a foundation year in which they may come in on a four-week attachment, or may have done their first year and be specialising in nursing children.

Enrolled nurse: the two-year enrolled training has now ceased. Enrolled nurses are encouraged to take the Registered Sick Children's Nurse qualifications.

Staff nurse: at the Children's Hospital almost all staff nurses are RSCNs. They have a greater degree of responsibility and deeper specialist knowledge.

Sister/charge nurse: sisters and their male equivalents, charge nurses, are the senior nurses on the wards and in theatre. They have 24-hour responsibility to ensure children on the wards get quality nursing care, and that the ward is run properly. They supervise the trained and student nurses.

Phlebotomist: a person who takes blood samples and carries out basic analysis of them.

Porter: a person who transports children and equipment around the hospital.

Domestic: a person who performs the essential task of keeping the hospital clean. Domestics make up the second largest workforce in the hospital, after nurses.

Social worker: a person who helps provide support for children and their families in the home.

Physiotherapist: a person who treats injury or disease with massage and exercises. Physiotherapists are heavily involved in the treatment of children with orthopaedic, muscular and respiratory conditions.

Speech therapist: a person who works to improve the speech of those with speech defects, e.g. as a result of a cleft palate.

Occupational therapist: a person who designs creative activities to aid a child's

recovery from certain illnesses.

Dietitian: a person trained in diet and nutrition who gives advice on eating to children with all sorts of condition – diabetes, Crohn's disease, food intolerances, etc.

Pharmacist: a person who prepares all the drug treatments and drips in the hospital.

Community nurse: a roving nurse who will assist families whose children require treatment in the home.

Drawing by Darren Redmond Age 15

Teacher: a person who is employed by the local education department to teach children who are in hospital for five days or more, and to teach sick children at home.

Chaplain: a person who is on call 24 hours a day, ministering to the spiritual needs of patients, their families and staff.

Jenny Walker
**Paediatric Consultant
Surgeon**

**Jenny Walker is one of the
hospital's three paediatric
consultant surgeons. You'll
find her either gowned up in
Theatre, running from ward to
ward, or half-way up a fell.
Any children in the region
who need complex surgery
may find their way into
Jenny's hands. As well as
operating in up to four
sessions a week, she shares
the job of training the next
generation of young
surgeons.**

There can't be many paediatric surgeons who drive a 1954 Land-Rover – still less in open-toed sandals, in all weathers. If the country does boast more than one they are unlikely to do the bulk of their own servicing, and are very unlikely to be a she.

Ask Jenny Walker what the link is between servicing a Land-Rover and operating on children, and she'll tell you: 'It's taking things to pieces very carefully and rebuilding them so they work better.' Couldn't be simpler, really . . .

Jenny joined the Children's Hospital's two other paediatric surgeons in January 1991. It's probably fair to say that, barring the odd game of squash or two summer weeks of competition sailing, she hasn't stopped since. A typical Theatre list might include removing a simple lump or cyst from a lad's neck, bowel surgery on a one-year-old baby or – more complex – rebuilding a child's waterworks 'that have got in a muddle'.

'Children make such wonderful patients. They're totally unpretentious. And they don't have any preconceived ideas about being ill. They just react to the way it is. It's the parents and grandparents who really suffer.' She explains that you have to treat the whole family in a children's hospital. The patient is the easy bit. 'When a little boy on the ward drives his tractor over your foot and shouts, "Move!" you can't help but smile. They make you human again, children.'

The 'Landy' will only do a top speed of 45mph (with the usual tail wind) on the way to her clinic in Grimsby, and Jenny herself travels at roughly the same pace walking through the hospital. She readily admits that her work demands a huge reserve of stamina (a glance at the diary shows the hours, sometimes day and night, she works), but she stresses that it's the team-work in hospital that really matters: not just the junior doctors and nurses who work for the three surgeons, but the porters, cooks and cleaners who make the place tick.

'What's so good about working in a small hospital is that everyone knows everyone else.' She's known for talking to a porter and the Chief Executive in exactly the same way.

When she was training to be a surgeon an older woman colleague advised her to give it up. A few years on Jenny doesn't deny that surgery is still a man's world. Sometimes parents ask her when the consultant is coming. When they realise they're talking to her some of them joke, 'a woman's stitching's bound to be better.'

Job satisfaction and enjoyment don't seem the right words when it comes to lack of sleep, or sharing anguish – or even great pain – with parents. But would she do anything else? 'Of course not.' ■

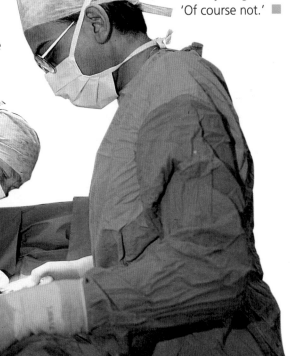

A Typical Day in Jenny Walker's Week

Monday

■	07.45ish	Sort through paperwork at the office. Dictate letters.
■	08.30	Check patients on wards, especially the neonates (babies in the first four weeks of life).
■	09.00	Theatre list. A 'mixed bag', all boys. Three-year-old with an undescended testicle, removal of kidney stones from a thirteen-year-old, implant ureters in right kidney of a three-year-old. Three operations fine.
■	12.45	Go to secretary's office, open mail. Sign letters while eating 'flying buttie' (tuna and mayonnaise), crisps and chocolate. Organise things from mail. Talk to colleagues about possibly needing to operate on an emergency admission.
■	16.00	Infection control committee. Bleeper goes off twice – about a baby on Ward 1.
■	17.30	Talk to junior staff on wards. More paperwork and dictation. See emergency admission: newborn baby with hernia. Arrange for Theatre. Postpone squash until Wednesday. Operate on baby.
■	20.00	Home, cook and eat. Three phone calls about the baby with hernia.
■	Midnight	Bed.

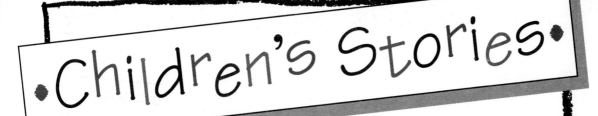

•Children's Stories•

. . . a lot better than I thought

Coming into hospital was a lot better than I thought. The nurses are all very kind. The ward is much smaller than I thought. I am glad that my mum could stay with me. I am glad I have had my operation. It did not hurt as much as I imagined. I was scared before I came in but not scared when I got here. Today I am waiting to go home. I wish it was now.

Thomas Shelton Age 10

when I Go into the hospital I go in the playroom and have lots of fun.

Alicia Fowler Age 5

I didn't like the operation
I do like the nurses

Timothy Age 5

Male and female nurses by
Chelsie Eccles Age 5

In Theatre

- There are three operating theatres at SCH. Each has an adjoining anaesthetics room. For over a century the number of operations carried out at the Children's Hospital has grown:

Year	Operations
1800	27
1900	234
1920	465
1940	630
1960	3731
1974	4262
1992	5394

- Each year the theatre staff get through:
  24 000 masks;
  21 600 hats;
  19 200 pairs of surgical gloves.
  All are worn by surgeons, anaesthetists, theatre sisters and nurses during operations.

- Some 667 980 centimetres of sutures are used each year for stitches (that's about 4.2 miles).

- Many of the surgeons listen to music while operating. Jenny Walker likes anything from Cat Stevens to the Rolling Stones. Mr Bull has a penchant for Vivaldi. Some, of course, prefer the Sound of Silence.

- Since 1977 the hospital has been doing day-case surgery. Some fifty children a week now have all-in-a-day surgery.

- Consultants who have at least one operating list at SCH:
  four plastic surgeons;
  six orthopaedic surgeons;
  three general paediatric surgeons;
  three dental surgeons;
  three ENT surgeons;
  eight anaesthetic consultants.

- There are twenty-nine theatre nurses (several of whom are part-time).

- There are seven operating department assistants (ODAs) who work in Theatre, set up and check anaesthetics equipment, assist in anaesthesia, check ventilators, are part of the resuscitation team and check all the resuscitation equipment in the hospital.

- Just three operating department orderlies ferried 5394 patients to Theatre last year.

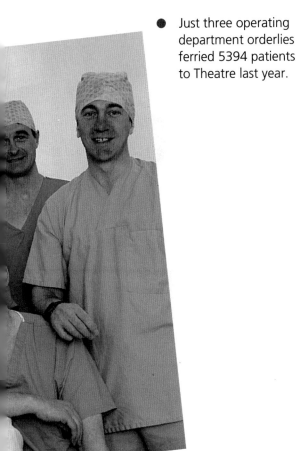

Theatre is a second home to the hospital anaesthetists.

Hernias

The repair of an inguinal hernia is the commonest operation performed on children. Each year over 200 are carried out in the hospital, the majority as a routine day case under a general anaesthetic. The hernia usually presents as a swelling in the groin when a baby cries or when older children run and jump about, and then disappears when they are quiet and still. It is more common in boys than girls. An umbilical hernia is a similar swelling at the navel or umbilicus but rarely needs an operation because it often resolves itself without any treatment.

Appendicitis

Appendicectomy for acute appendicitis is the most frequently performed emergency operation. About 100 are done each year, but many more children are admitted to hospital for observation to exclude appendicitis. It is unusual under five years of age and can sometimes be very difficult to diagnose but, typically, the child looks flushed, has a mild fever and complains of a colicky stomach pain with loss of appetite. This is accompanied by vomiting before the pain settles low down on the right-hand side. Most children go home three to four days after the operation.

Children's Stories

Laura's Story

Laura Norris is a veteran of Ward 7. Born with short bowel syndrome, she is five years old and going strong. Her mother Jill writes about their time at the Children's Hospital.

I don't know how many times I have sat here awaiting Laura's safe return from Theatre; I stopped counting when they reached double figures some years ago. Theatre is a place where, as a parent, you have no control over your child. But today Laura went with no fuss, as if it was an everyday occurrence.

This time it was a minor operation just to remove a blocked Broviac [vascular access catheter], but it was a new experience for Laura because the anaesthetist could not find a vein to put her to sleep and she had to have the 'magic wind'.

Her short life seems to have revolved around the Children's Hospital. I often wonder who the nurses are actually here for – certainly not just for the children, because without their care, love and understanding as a parent I would have gone crazy. It seems very unfair that good health in this country is seen as luck rather than a right. We expect the best for our children with some of the best doctors in the world, but they don't have the funds to research new techniques or the money for new equipment.

I am not complaining about Laura's care; she's always had the best, and whenever she has required surgery it's as if she's been the surgeon's own child. A more caring and skilled man could not be found.

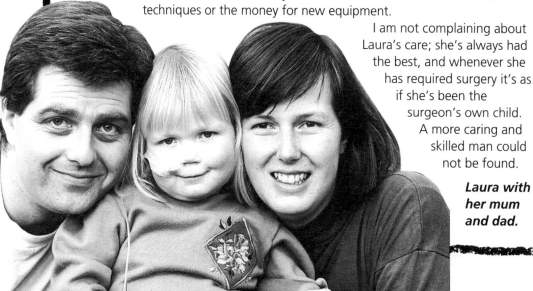

Laura with her mum and dad.

Laura has changed our family life 100 per cent, bringing great joy as a positive, bright, happy child, yet sadness with the frequent hospital admissions and the problems that this brings. Ask her what her biggest achievement is and I am sure she would say going to big school, which she started two days ago; being accepted as an equal, as she has been, is very important to her. She has already made new friends who make no comment about the tube in her nose or the fact that they are all at least head and shoulders above her. The only person to worry was a dinner lady who wanted to know why a child of about three was playing in the school yard! This was soon sorted out when her older sister Gemma explained.

Laura is five years old, and in the last three weeks she has started to try to hop and run – but only a few steps before she falls. The smile on her face is a joy.

It's hard not to be able to answer her questions about the future. 'Will I need this tube when I am a lady?' is the one she is asking the most, but we just don't know. Her greatest joy is horse riding; I hope she never asks for her own horse!

The ward phone is ringing; she is in recovery, so I run the now familiar route to her. She is sitting on the nurse's knee, arms outstretched for her mummy. Thank you once again, everyone, for her safe return.

Short Bowel Syndrome

Typically, a baby is born with 120–300 cm (4–10 ft) of small intestine. Any baby with less than 80 cm (2 ft 8 in) may have problems with absorbing enough food. Those with less than 20 cm (8 in) will have problems and have what is known as short bowel syndrome. These babies are unlikely to manage on normal feeds. A short bowel may be caused by the bowel growing abnormally, an injury to it, or a disease after birth. Most babies with more than 20 cm will eventually 'adapt' and learn to absorb enough food as they grow. However, children with less than 20 cm face a life of intravenous feeding and may suffer from the effects of liver failure, which is often a secondary problem. One solution may be an operation to divide the bowel lengthways and suture it so as to narrow it but double its length. Small bowel transplantation has been performed and, if combined with new drugs that prevent rejection of the bowel, these children may survive to lead a normal life.

Children's Stories

Lisa's Story

Lisa Flinders has Crohn's Disease, an inflammatory bowel disease which can cause lack of appetite, poor absorption of food, poor growth and general malaise.

Hi! I'm Lisa. I've got Crohn's Disease and had it since I was a baby. Since then I've been in and out of hospital. It's been a lot worse in the last couple of years. I had an operation in October 1990 and another in March 1993.

When you're in hospital as much as I am you get to know a lot of people. I know all the Ward 4 staff, the physio Dave, the night sisters, most of the porters and lots of staff and doctors from other wards.

When you first go into the ward they may let you pick your own bed. When you've got your bed, a nurse will come and ask some questions about yourself and what you like to do, and take your temperature with a special machine, take your pulse by holding your wrist and take your blood pressure by putting a cuff on your arm which is connected by a wire to a big machine. After, they'll ask you if you want a drink or something to eat.

If you need to go on any special machines, like I always have to, the nurse will show you how it works and how to set it up. When you've got settled, you can look round and meet the nursery nurse. She'll get you a game or some drawing paper and crayons.There is also a teacher who comes round.

There's lots you can do in hospital. You can choose what you want to eat because they bring you a menu round unless you are on a special diet like I am, then the nurse will get you a dietitian and she will sort you something out. Also, if you get hungry you can ask the nurse for something and if they haven't got anything on the ward that you fancy they'll fill in a form and see if they've got any in the kitchen. They also let relatives bring you sweets and things.

When you walk round the ward you may notice that some children have signs above their beds that say PLEASE DO NOT GIVE ME ANYTHING TO EAT OR DRINK. That means that they'll be having a test or an operation done.

In hospital I've made a lot of friends and keep in touch with them. Maybe you will too.

Lisa Flinders Age 11

Football Crazy . . .

Lisa Flinders is mad about Sheffield Wednesday. The Hillsborough stand towers over her home, just a goal kick away from the main gate. She has long dreamt of being a mascot for the team. This season, as they marched to two cup finals, her chance came. A letter came from the club asking her to lead out Chris Waddle, Carlton Palmer, Chris Woods and the boys on 24 March. But Lisa was due an operation for her Crohn's disease at around that time. The club pulled the date forward to 13 February. In the week before the match, Lisa sprained her ankle – playing football. Would she be ready for the big day? On Friday, with less than 24 hours to go, her plaster was taken off. Lisa was pronounced match fit.

On the big day Lisa walked round the corner to the ground, where she was given a signed football. Then, shortly before the match began, she was taken into the changing rooms to give the lads a bit of pre-match advice. It's not often females are allowed to go in there.

Just before three o'clock, a roar went up, and Lisa led the teams down the tunnel and out on to the pitch – in front of 30 000 spectators. 'Today's mascot – Lisa Flinders', flashed the scoreboard. After a photo session with John Harkes and shaking hands with the referee, Lisa retired to the touchline.

A great day for Lisa. But was she a lucky mascot? Of course – the final score was Sheffield Wednesday 2, Southend 0.

Kath Hurst and Rita Taylor
Domestics

Rita Taylor (left) and Kathleen Hurst (right) are the hospital's best double act. As domestics, they've been together for eighteen years – a key part of the second largest workforce in the hospital, after the nurses. Once they cleaned by daylight, but for the last six years they have only come out at night.

Kath and Rita go back a long way. In the eighteen years they have been together, Rita has only had one day off sick. At the dead of night, while everyone sleeps, this night-time duo can be found cleaning, scrubbing and keeping each other company. They leave home just before 10 p.m. to start work and don't get back till 7 a.m. the following morning.

During the night they will have polished floors and stairs, damp-dusted the theatres and negotiated their way around children and parents who've had to come into Accident and Emergency.

It may seem unglamorous work but, with germs and bacteria circulating, keeping the place clean is among the most important jobs in the hospital. Scrubbing the theatres is specialised work. Like the surgeons they clean up after, they have to wear gowns, gloves and surgical caps. They take great pride in their job, but often find time for a laugh, a joke and (most nights) a song. So used to working together, they have become a double act – they even finish off each other's sentences.

When asked if their respective husbands mind them working such anti-social hours they both laugh. Rita, tongue in cheek, says: 'No, no. My husband's bought a rubber dolly to keep him company at night.'

After nearly two decades of keeping the building clean, Rita and Kath are among the hospital's least seen but longest serving staff. ∎

Matching the right number of children to the number of beds available is a balancing act. In theory it's straightforward. In practice it can be anything but. Chris recalls wistfully the days when 'there was a bed waiting for each child with his or her name on it. Now the bed's likely to be still warm!' The hospital tries to pitch the number of beds and nurses to meet requirements: 126 beds are 'open' for use but a further forty are 'closed' at present because there isn't the money to staff them.

So just after 9 a.m., as children arrive outside the door, Anne, Chris or Judith may discover that the allocated beds are already occupied. Then begins a frenzied period of juggling. Are any beds on other wards free? Is anyone ready for discharge? Can an operation be done as a day case and so save a bed?

Usually, with skilful shuffling, a bed can be found somewhere. It's a point of pride. 'We've only had to cancel children once this year. We usually manage to squeeze them in,' says Anne.

Occasionally a child must wait, and not all parents are understanding: 'One dad thought we were doing it on purpose. You can under-stand – we have kids ourselves. Parents take time off work. Many stand to lose money.'

With over fifty years experience of the National Health Service between them, Anne, Chris and Judith rarely get flustered, even when it seems there are just too many children and too few beds. 'We thrive on it,' says Anne. 'Must have a certain sort of madness within us, I suppose.' ■

Admissions

'Hello, admissions . . .' It's nine o'clock in the morning and the phones are buzzing. Parents of children due in for treatment are ringing to make sure there is a bed for their child. It's beds that keep Chris Naish (left), Anne Toseland (centre) and Judith Watson (right) busy. Only they know exactly what the 'bed state' is – who's in, who's gone home, and how many empty beds there are in the hospital.

31

Carrie McKenzie
Senior Registrar and Medical Lecturer

Singing star of the Junior Doctors' Revue and keen hockey player, Carrie McKenzie still finds the time to be a medical lecturer and senior registrar at the Children's Hospital. Carrie is one of the small band of Scots that have migrated to Sheffield.

Profile • Profile •

Carrie had recently finished her 'O' levels and was trying to work out what to do in the sixth form. 'Mum said, "At some point you have to decide what you want to be." I said, "I think I want to be a doctor." It took me as much by surprise as it did her.'

Now Carrie is one notch below getting the elusive job of a consultant, the last step up the ladder in hospital medicine. She's climbed it fast – she was only twenty-seven when she first got her present job. Hard junior doctor hours haven't diminished her energy for medicine or for life outside.

'I try to work hard and play hard – and that doesn't mean I drink a lot!' In Carrie's case what it does mean is getting up before 7 a.m. most mornings, and swimming forty or so lengths before checking the wards. In season she plays hockey twice a week. This year she has also taken the lead in the Junior Doctors' Revue and planned the small matter of her wedding.

Building a relationship with the parents and patients in hospital is what gives her most satisfaction in her work, whether the illness is trivial or serious. Earning parents' trust is a crucial skill when it comes to helping families with a child who has a long-term illness such as diabetes or asthma.

And the future for Dr McKenzie? Not surprisingly, she wants to break new ground for Sheffield and manage to get a job-share consultancy as a physician. That way Carrie and a colleague can stay in hospital medicine and have time to bring up a family. ■

Carrie McKenzie's Diary
Week beginning 8 March 1993

Monday
Up at **6.30 a.m.** to swim before work.

At the hospital before **8 a.m.** to see 'who and where' the patients are before the X-ray conference and ward round begin.

10 a.m. Consultant ward round. The team (but not me) have been on call this weekend so quite a few patients to be seen, investigations to arrange and results to chase. Busy morning.

2 p.m. Tutorial with the medical students as part of their revision course *but* poor attendance considering the proximity of their exam. Sadly the session was interrupted by several bleeps from the ward.

3.45 p.m. Ward round to review the children hoping to go home and to check results of today's tests, speak to parents and generally leave things in order.

6.30 p.m. Just enough time to get over to the sports centre in time for the hockey selection committee meeting to sort out Saturday's teams, etc. Numerous problems with selection for the weekend because of injuries, unavailable players and clashing fixtures. As ever, no umpires!

Home about **8.30 p.m.** to find Warren and his friends avidly watching the football – FA Cup 6th round – the perfect excuse to retire to the relaxing sanctuary of the study to get on with preparation for my thesis viva and Friday's presentation.

Thankfully Sheffield Wednesday manage to draw with Derby County. In bed by **11 p.m.**!

Tuesday *(on call)*
Few early swimmers this morning so plenty of room to swim.

Today – just casualty to cover and the wards to sort out! No major problems, so time to go through exam technique with the medical students.

12.30 p.m. Junior staff meeting with the consultants and really very few grumbles or problems.

A rather frustrating afternoon spent trying both to empty beds and move children around to allow new admissions access to beds.

4 p.m. Research seminar on bone aging and adult height prediction, but interrupted by frequent bleeps to casualty.

5.30 – 6.00 p.m. Hand-overs from the other teams and a quick tour of the wards and ICU [Intensive Care Unit] to review the sickest children and make sure all is well.

Remarkably (and ominously) quiet evening all round so, after an hour or so at my desk, home for supper with Warren.

Still all quiet at bedtime but at **2 a.m.** urgent call to casualty to see a child with 'difficulty breathing' – epiglotitis on ICU.

As ever, once in the hospital at night there are other children to see and parents to reassure.

Bed at **6.30 a.m.**, very tired! (No point in going home, so short sleep snatched in the on-call room.)

Wednesday
Up at **7.30 a.m.** to sort out Mark's insulin before breakfast. Quick round to make sure there are no immediate problems on the wards before the consultant ward round at **9 a.m.** Despite a long night there are few patients to see – the child with epiglotitis is doing well on ICU.

After the ward round a much-needed cup of coffee to sort out who is doing what from the round and then back to the office to sort out the backlog of admin. before Diabetic Clinic at **2 p.m.**

Thankfully, the clinic is not too busy today and finishes at **4 p.m.** – time to catch up!

Jonathan's repeat head scan looks a bit worrying and needs a neurosurgical opinion – the neurosurgeon cannot come over to the Children's Hospital until evening.

The orthopaedic surgeons want us to take over the care of one of their patients with a swollen foot. Unfortunately, I cannot explain the situation to her parents who speak only Urdu, so an interpreter, in the shape of a junior doctor from the same part of their country, is found.

Home at last soon after **7 p.m.** and too late (and too tired) to go hockey training or for that matter do anything else.

So – a leisurely bath, clean clothes and across the road to the pub for supper before bed and sleep by **9 p.m.**!

Thursday (on call)
Great difficulty in believing it's time to get up when the alarm rings *but* nevertheless at the Health Club by **7 a.m.**

My bleeper was bleeping as I arrived, query the dose of insulin prescribed for Mark before his breakfast, and so the day begins and continues with a succession of clinical problems to solve. Start ward round but frequent visits to casualty as four children need admission.

Good news on Jonathan's brain scan: he does not need any surgical attention.

Jayne is having her tonsils removed tomorrow and needs her diabetic regime organised around theatre times – understandably, she's apprehensive about the anaesthetic.

Casualty was bedlam all evening (Thursday is often busy because many GPs have a half day). Warren brought in some Chinese food but I'm afraid there was no time to stop and eat.

Finally, home at **3 a.m.** and no further calls before the alarm rings at **7 a.m.**

Friday
No swim today – on call until **9 a.m.**

• Diary • Diary •

Early ward round before handing over to Ann and making off to the station to catch the **9.28 a.m.** to London St Pancras for all-day meeting.

Saturday

Up early to get various 'jobs' done before playing hockey. Flowers ordered for the wedding and details of the menu checked for reception.

11.15 a.m. Meet for a 12.00 match – last league game of the season. Blistering hot day (for this early in the season!). 4 – 0 defeat but nevertheless fun; time for a drink in the sunshine with 'the girls' after the match before getting on with some work on my thesis.

Sunday

Up very early – not by design, but woke early and couldn't get back to sleep. Early start in my study on the thesis and made good progress.

Breakfast with Warren before he set off for work and I settled back into my study for the morning.

Lunch at the pub in the village before going to Hillsborough to see Sheffield Wednesday beat Blackburn in the FA Cup. Stopped off to help friend move some furniture before afternoon tea at Warren's parents.

A long evening with my thesis!! ■

Asthma

- Asthma is a very common problem in childhood; diagnosed by a history of recurrent cough and wheeze.

- In Britain it is estimated that 30 per cent of children have an episode of wheeze at some time and 10–15 per cent will have recurrent wheeze.

- Asthma appears to be twice as common in boys as girls. This sex difference disappears in adolescence.

- A tendency to asthma may be inherited.

- Viral infections are by far the most common cause of an asthma attack but cigarette smoke, pollen, house dust, pets, food, medicines, exercise, emotional factors and changes in the weather may all bring on symptoms.

- In most children asthma can be treated quite simply by using a variety of medicines which are more effective if inhaled rather than swallowed.

- While there is no 'cure' for asthma, current treatment is very effective with few side-effects. Asthma should be seen more as an inconvenience than a disease.

Children's Stories

Becky Vickers' Story

Last week I went to the doctors because I wasn't feeling well. I was thirsty and had lots of headaches and I'd lost a lot of weight. Me and my mum had gone to see what was wrong. My doctor took a blood test and he sent it away to be tested. He asked us to come back in two days. We came back and he told me I had Diabetes and me and my mum had to go to hospital. We got on the bus and I felt rather unhappy. When the bus stopped outside the hospital we got off and went straight to Ward 4. I didn't know what to expect. I met the nurse Neil. I also met a B.B.C. camera crew and I didn't expect that! I met Dr. Wales and another boy who had Diabetes. We had a long chat. I went to sit on my bed and Pam Sparkes the diabetic nurse came and talked to me. She showed me some needles and how to inject insulin. It didn't seem that bad, and then came the blood-tests. The blood-tests are the worst part about having Diabetes. Pam told me I would have to inject insulin for the rest of my life. This was quite a shock at first but now I have got used to it. I also met Frances the dietitian and we talked. Frances had some plastic food which I thought was brill. I have to count out my food in portions. The good news is I can still eat everything I like. The great news is I've GOT to have little snacks before exercise and in between meals. I thought I might have to stop in hospital but I didn't. I have been back a few times since and the doctors are helping me get my insulin dose right. Since I started the insulin I feel a lot better.

Becky Vickers Age 10

Drawing by Becky Vickers

Diabetes

- Diabetes is the name given to a condition in which the pancreas does not make enough insulin. It affects roughly 1 in 500 children in the UK.

- Sugar, in the form of glucose, is the main fuel used by the body to provide energy.

- Insulin is like a key to open the door of the body's cells and allow glucose to enter.

- In diabetes, lack of insulin allows glucose to accumulate in the blood and spill out into the urine, making the child go to the toilet more often and causing thirst and weight loss.

- We do not really understand what causes diabetes, although there is much research in progress.

- Sometimes children who develop it have relatives in their family who also have diabetes.

- Diabetes is not caused by eating the wrong things and is not 'caught' from others.

- The only way to treat diabetes in childhood is by daily injections of insulin.

- Insulin cannot be taken as tablets as they would be destroyed by the stomach's juices.

- Important factors in treating diabetes are a healthy diet and exercise.

- Complications of diabetes are rare in childhood; later in life, if the blood sugar is not carefully controlled, problems will develop with the eyes, kidneys and feet.

- Children have this condition for many years, making it important that they look after their diabetes to ensure good health in the future.

•Children's Stories•

Natasha Banks' Story

I am Natasha Banks. I am nineteen years old, come from Cudworth in Barnsley – and am proud of it. I was born with cystic fibrosis (CF). It is a genetically inherited disease for which there is yet no cure – but we are hopeful for the future. I also have diabetes which was caused by my CF. For me to carry on and live a normal life, I desperately need a new heart and lungs. I was accepted on to the Papworth list nearly twelve months ago, and have carried a bleeper since. During this time I have, with lots of help from my mum and dad, worked extremely hard to keep myself well enough for a transplant.

I have physiotherapy three or four times daily which moves the thick mucus in my lungs. I take around fifty tablets a day, because I cannot absorb food as well as other people. I have two insulin injections a day, and more recently have had to have intravenous antibiotics every four to eight weeks, which is not nice. I feel let down because my bleeper has only gone off once, and that was because it was flat. Everyone who dies and doesn't have their organs donated is wasted, and they could help save someone else's life.

The problem with CF is that you look normal on the outside, so people think you are well – we have all our limbs, and can walk. Our treatment is not pleasant. I think if it made your hair fall out more people would want to help us.

When you are out and have a coughing bout and need to spit, people are ignorant and look at you as if they are going to catch something.

The above words are Natasha's own, dictated to me, as her disease had progressed too far for her to write.

Natasha sadly died before we completed her story, but Dot and Roy, her parents, still wanted it to go in the book as it was her wish. Natasha hoped her contribution might encourage organ donation.

Her death does not end Natasha's story. Natasha always wanted to donate her own organs in the event of her death and her parents carried out her brave wishes. Eight children have been given the chance to improve their lives. I know Natasha would wish them well.

CHRIS WARD
Community Nurse

Cystic Fibrosis

- CF is the most commonly inherited life-threatening disease in this country.
- It clogs the lungs with mucus and attacks the digestive system.
- As yet there is no cure.
- One person in every twenty-five carries the CF gene.
- Two million people in the UK are carriers.
- For parents who both carry the defective gene, there is a one-in-four chance with each pregnancy that their baby will have CF.
- There is a one-in-two chance that the baby will be completely healthy, but a carrier.
- There is a one-in-four chance that the baby will be completely free of CF and not even a carrier.
- Six thousand people in the UK have cystic fibrosis.
- Three people die every week because of CF.

Food

It's 6.30 in the morning and the kitchens are already a hubbub of activity. Cooks in blue check trousers and white overalls whistle as they begin preparing the day's lunches – up to 150 for the children and a further 300 for the staff and visitors.

'It's special working in a children's hospital. Sometimes the kids come down to visit us and see what we're doing – they're always welcome,' says Lee, who, as the saying goes, probably *has* cooked more hot dinners . . . He has also dressed up as Chippie the Bear and gone round the wards to ask children what they think of their meals.

The cooks, nine of them on a rota to cover teas and lunches, prepare a staggering 4000 meals a week. The children's menus are set in consultation with the hospital's dietitians, to make sure they are nutritionally balanced. No foods with artificial additives, preservatives or colours are used, and ingredients are low sugar and, where possible, salt free. Orders from the menus are phoned down by the nurses from each ward every morning.

But the children always come first. 'Whatever they want, they can have,' says Amanda, the Assistant Catering Manager, firmly. 'If they're feeling poorly, they won't feel like eating much anyway, so we try to provide them with whatever they fancy. At least then they eat something.' If children don't want the 'official' menu, the cooks will try and prepare whatever they do want. Special requests are usually in the burger, fish finger, chicken nuggets line, and chips with everything! 'It's particularly important for the children on Ward 3, the cancer ward, where the chemotherapy really puts them off their food.'

But they also believe in fun in the food department. 'If it's a child's birthday, the nurses ring down and let us know and we make a specially decorated birthday cake with the child's name on and a party tea, with jellies, sticky buns and sausage rolls, for the whole ward,' says Amanda. 'We do the same at Easter and Christmas – makes it a bit of a treat.'

Examples of food to eat sparingly – in plastic.

Lunch

Main course
Salmon fishcake and parsley sauce
or Lasagne
or Vegetarian dish
Vegetables
Creamed potatoes
or Croquette potatoes
Peas
Mixed vegetables

Sweet
Coconut tart and custard
or A fresh orange

Dinner

Jacket potato with baked beans and grated cheese
or Egg salad
or Ham sandwiches

Sweet
Muesli slice *or* Strawberry jelly

Lunch

Main course
Roast chicken
or Beef curry
or Minced chicken in gravy
or Vegetarian dish
Vegetables
Boiled rice
or Duchess potatoes
Cabbage
Green Beans

Sweet
Chocolate sponge and chocolate sauce
or A fresh apple

Dinner

Sausage and spaghetti
or Turkey salad
or Cream cheese and cucumber sandwiches

Sweet
Peaches and cream *or* Ice cream

The kitchens also provide the wards with little extras – supplies of Ribena and orange juice for the children to drink whenever they want. Between them, the ten wards consume sixty-six bottles of Ribena a week!

As an enterprising extra, they run a Flying Butty service. Staff and visitors alike can ring the kitchens with an order, and at noon, your sandwich, handmade by the canteen staff, will be whizzed to any corner of the hospital.

41

Ugh! Take it away. It makes me ill.

Some children are not so lucky with food. For reasons that aren't clear, when they have egg or cow's milk or certain other foods they have a very bad reaction.

A few facts about food intolerance:

- The hospital's dietitian sees an average of twenty children every month for food intolerance, five of whom are new patients.

- Milk, eggs, nuts, wheat and food additives are the substances most likely to cause problems.

- Symptoms vary from child to child: they may include skin rashes, swelling, vomiting, diarrhoea and wheezing. Treatment involves identifying the problem food and then excluding it from the diet, usually for at least six months.

- Cow's milk intolerance is the most common food intolerance. Replacing the cow's milk with soya usually solves the problem.

- A small percentage of young children who have had to switch to soya become intolerant of that as well.

- Multiple food intolerances are uncommon. They should always be treated under the supervision of a doctor and dietitian to ensure that the diet is appropriate and nutritionally adequate.

- Many children grow out of their food intolerances, often by the age of two. For others, symptoms may become less severe and their restricted diet can be relaxed.

Hospital Food   Jonathan Pearson

I do not like hospital food because it is not the same as mummys. I think it is too soft. I like the Jelly, bread and coca cola. I dont like Jacket potato Sausage and tomatoes!

I like

I dont like

Michael Ogden's Story

Sally Ogden writes about the challenge of feeding her son, Michael.

On 4 June 1991 I gave birth to a healthy baby boy – or so it seemed. Michael's problem couldn't be seen from the outside. After breast-feeding him for five weeks, I had to take Michael to SCH with diarrhoea and screaming. The doctors didn't know why he was in pain and started a series of tests.

Michael was put on to soya milk. The doctors told me he had an intolerance to my milk. I felt as though I had been poisoning him and that I had really let him down. But it was wonderful to see him free from pain and smiling. Then at five months he had to go back into hospital. He wouldn't eat anything. Just the sight of his bottles of soya milk started him screaming. He was losing weight. The doctors discovered he was allergic to soya. By seven months, Michael had several more intolerances. By now he was on a milk-free, soya-free, wheat-free, gluten-free and egg-free diet. Finding food which Michael could eat and contained enough calories was almost impossible.

We badly needed support. Without Frances, our dietitian at the hospital, our GP and chemist, we couldn't have coped. Then, at the age of thirteen months, one by one, Michael was put back on to soya, wheat, gluten and milk. That just left egg. The final hurdle came on 11 February – the egg challenge. In the three hours on day care from a scratch test with egg white and yolk to a plateful of scrambled eggs on toast – he sailed through.

Now he goes to toddler group, 'gym-tots', walks and swims twice a week. All we can say is thank you, SCH!

Jacquie Purkiss
Physiotherapist

Jacquie is a physiotherapist specialising in work with children who have had major surgery on their legs. Sheffield is one of the few national centres for the treatment of children who are short in stature or have limb inequality – that is, one leg longer than the other. Surgery involves breaking the bone, fixing an appliance to the two halves and stretching it very slowly over a number of months as it heals. All being well, short-stature children end up taller; those with limb inequality end up with legs much closer in length.

Jacquie has a warning for every child who is going to have their leg length-ened: 'You're going to shout at me, you're probably going to hate me. But we've got to start physio as soon as we can after the operation. Otherwise there's not much chance of success.'

She explains: 'The operation breaks the bone. The fixator holds it in place. Turning the keys on the fixator starts to widen the gap. It stretches the bone slowly, slowly, teasing it out like a ball of cotton wool. In that tug of war it's easy for the bones to go one way and the muscles to go the other.' So the aim of her work is to stretch the muscles very slowly, to get them used to the longer limb. It can be painful.

She has a repertoire of jokes and stories to match the job. 'I enjoy making the kids laugh, taking their mind off what looks like torture and what, at times, must feel like torture. That's the challenge. I might tease quite a loud lad and be gentler with someone who's a bit shy. The trick's to get the whole family's confidence from the start, because it's the fear of what I'm going to do as much as any therapy that worries them.'

The daughter of a famous Kilmarnock goalkeeper, she can hold her own with the cockiest of lads. But the tough tomboy exterior hides a 'big softie' – her own words. 'I was taught at physio school never to get involved emotionally. But you can't help but get involved with the kids some-times. After a difficult session when they're

• Profile • Profile

off thinking, "That big witch, I just hate her," it's not easy. I've been known to go away and have a good cry. But we always make up next time.'

Spring is a particularly busy time for Jacquie. It's the lead-up time to the annual summer ball. She's been involved in organising it since it began, four years ago, and it's a huge amount of work. Booking the venue, arranging the dinner, organising the tombola and bingo, collecting prizes from local firms for the raffle, selling tickets . . . This year she's been developing her juggling skills. On top of her regular physio work and all the planning for this annual event, she's expecting her first baby. The orthopaedics ward have confidently predicted it'll arrive the day of the ball. ■

Jacquie and a 'leg-lengthener' at work.

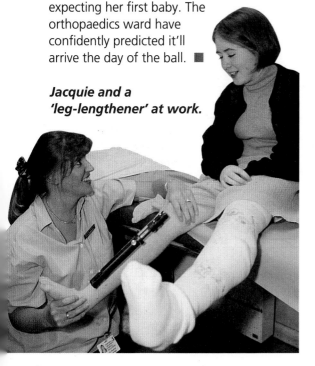

Leg Lengthening

● Sheffield Children's Hospital is a national centre for the treatment of limb inequality (one leg longer than the other), short-stature children and children with leg deformity.

● On the basis of work pioneered in Russia and Italy, surgeons Mr Saleh and Mr Bell have refined the technique for lengthening limbs (mainly legs).

● Surgery involves 'breaking' the bone and using pins to attach a fixator to the bone on either side of the break. By turning screws 1 mm a day the fixator lengthens and 'grows' the bone as it heals.

● The maximum growth achieved is 20–25 cm (8–10 in).

● Limb lengthening often involves more than one operation.

● Preparation before the operation and physiotherapy afterwards are vital if the treatment is to succeed.

● Children wear the fixators for three to twelve months.

● To date, approximately 150 children have had this new surgery at the hospital.

Children's Stories

Jonathan Archer's Story

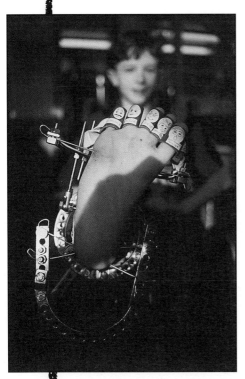

Jonathan is ten years old and a keen footballer. He was born with tallipes (club foot) and came into hospital for a foot 'correction'.

I didn't enjoy doing physio at first because my foot hurt too much and moving my foot was painful. The exercises were quite difficult, but Jacquie helped me along. If I was finding a particular exercise painful, I'd finish that exercise and then Jacquie would talk to me about things she's done or have happened to her.

On one occasion she told me about when she went hunting Haggis. She said that they have four legs, but on one side of their bodies they have shorter legs than on the other, so they can run around the hills where they live. Another time she tried to teach me to speak Scottish. She taught me to say, 'It's a braw bricht moonlicht nicht thi nicht – awe richt,' whatever that means!

When she knew I was interested in football, she told me that her father used to play in goal for Kilmarnock (they're in the Scottish First Division). Every time I turned up for physio she would say, 'Did you know my father used to play for Kilmarnock?' She said it every day until it became a private joke.

Once in the hospital, Dad mimicked Jacquie in a Scottish accent while I was doing physio, and the girl in the bed opposite me was laughing at him. It was really funny.

Altogether, Jacquie is very helpful when you're finding exercises difficult. She is a good laugh and is good at telling stories!

Jonathan's Mum Judy Writes:

Mr Saleh and Jonathan Pagdin did everything possible to prepare us as a family for the operation. They showed us photographs of metal frames and we met a couple of people undergoing similar treatment.

But no one can prepare you for the amount of pain that follows an operation like this. Mr Saleh assured us that everything had gone well and told us that Jonathan would need a lot of support from us over the next few days. I didn't appreciate what that meant until a few hours later when Jonathan was in terrible, relentless pain.

It was like entering a long dark tunnel. During those first days I actually regretted the operation, because the amount of pain he was experiencing seemed to be beyond reasonable limits. I remember thinking, 'What on earth have I done? This is a big mistake.' In fact, the first week is a blur of intense pain, exhaustion and anxiety. Jonathan slept very little for the first two nights and, as I was sharing the side ward with him, I hardly slept either.

The feeling of helplessness in the face of such suffering was perhaps the worst part. I remember times when Jonathan had cried so much he was exhausted and all I could do was hold him.

I really wondered how I was going to get through this time and was afraid that Jonathan would never accept his frame. On the second day, a very experienced nurse took me into the bathroom, put her arms around me and let me cry on her shoulder, while she reassured me that I was doing well and that Jonathan *would* get better. I really appreciated her care and for noticing that I needed support too.

Three months on, Jonathan's foot has changed remarkably. He is without pain and, thankfully, has accepted the frame. Very soon he is to try to walk on the frame, which is a positive encouragement that the healing process is well underway, and makes the difficult times worthwhile.

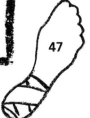

•Children's Stories•

Jenny Longbottom's Story

Jenny Longbottom is mother of Gillian, aged fourteen, who has come into hospital for her leg-lengthening treatment.

In 1984 my daughter, aged six, my husband and myself came to Sheffield Children's Hospital out-patient orthopaedic clinic from Cambridgeshire. In January 1993 Gillian underwent orthopaedic surgery to help her legs grow. She has achondroplasia, restricted growth or dwarfism. Her legs have not grown normally and the leg-lengthening team at Sheffield have offered her the chance of growing up to eight inches.

Cartoon by Gillian Longbottom Age 14

We waited a long time, were assessed, prepared, assured, informed and, above all, warned of the sheer strain, commitment and patience required to undergo limb lengthening, and we went ahead!

Gillian has now achieved three inches of length since January. The time has been long, arduous, stressful, incredibly worrying; the immobility boring and tearful; the pain severe at first – but we are still proceeding. I have been happy, vivacious, well controlled, calm and relaxed for Gillian's sake. But there were times when I needed to cry, needed to tell someone that I couldn't cope, wanted them to stop and give me back my happy, smiling child and we would go home and forget it. At those times the staff on Ward 5 were always there, and the physiotherapist Jacquie was there to listen until we decided to carry on.

We have a long, long way to go before this procedure is over. We have put ourselves in the hands of the limb-lengthening team and the care of SCH, and they have been there to help – to make us laugh again, but above all, to offer Gillian the opportunity to grow a little more and improve the quality of her life.

Profile • Profile

A childhood accident sparked Steve Taylor's interest in nursing. 'I was thirteen when I broke my arm severely. I was swinging on a tree above a quarry. I fell 30 feet but luckily landed on my arm, not my head. It was so bad I nearly lost my arm. When I got off the floor my arm was 90 degrees from my hand.' After four operations on his radius and ulna, Steve's arm did recover, but he still has the scars. It left him with a fascination for hospitals. When Steve left school nursing seemed the obvious thing to do.

By way of Doncaster, and 'Jimmy's' in Leeds, Steve arrived in Sheffield. He enjoys running a relaxed ward, where children are normally in for some time. The corridor is used for wheelchair races, or toy darts.

Those spending time on Ward 5 commonly have fractures – from football, climbing, skateboards and road accidents. There are also children undergoing leg-lengthening (an SCH speciality) and spinal fusion, and babies with tallipes (club feet) or congenital hip problems. ■

Steve Taylor

Steve Taylor is one of three Charge Nurses in the hospital. He runs the Orthopaedic Ward.

Last year Ward 5 saw the following broken bones:

46 skulls	1 collarbone
19 noses	12 hands
3 jaws	79 legs
1 spine	12 ankles
3 ribs	3 feet
5 pelvises	242 arms

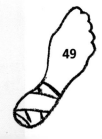

·Children's Stories·

Work and Play . . .

My stay in hospital began when I came in for pins in my right leg. On a morning I get up at 8.00 a.m. I have my breakfast when I get up then I get a wash, get ready and my day begins.

I have physio with Jacquie in the gym. Some of the exercises I do are painful but Jacquie says it's to make my leg better.

Then I clean my pins, firstly massaging them. Then I clean the wound and pins with cotton buds and sterile water, making sure my hands are clean at all times. After cleaning my pins I go on my CPM [Continuous Passive Movement] machine for four hours a day.

Gareth Conlen Age 11

Drawing by Andrew Ridsdale

Claire
Nursery Nurse.

I came into hospital on Monday morning.
I came into hospital because I had an injury on my knee.
I have to take antibiotics through a needle in my hand.
At first I felt upset.
But when I got in a ward I felt a lot better, because the first thing I did was have a water fight.
They took some pus off my knee in theatre while I was asleep.
The doctors and nurses are like my friends at school and at home.
The best thing here is that you can do anything you want, and there are lots of toys and games to choose from.
The worst thing I think will be leaving, although I look forward to seeing my pets.

Daniel Marsden Age 9

Children's Stories

. . . on the Ward

I don't like it in bed, but I like it in the wheelchair. I like riding around in my wheelchair with my friend Gareth. I like the nurses. I also like supper and breakfast.

I get up and have my breakfast and then go in my wheelchair and then I do my schoolwork with the hospital teacher, which I like. I like to go and play in the playroom.

Andrew Ridsdale Age 8

Drawing by Andrew Ridsdale

51

Martin Coleman
Senior Radiographer

Martin Coleman is not surprised to be the hospital's first male radiographer. He was the first man to do the job at both of London's specialist children's hospitals: Queen Elizabeth's in Hackney and Great Ormond Street. When he started out, he only ever planned to work in X-ray for a couple of years. Eighteen years on, he still buzzes with enthusiasm.

Profile • Profile

'**K**ids rarely pretend they're sick when they're not. They're honest to the point of being blunt. And you can't assume they'll do what you tell them. Each one's a challenge, and you only get one chance to get it right.'

Whether Martin is X-raying a lad's suspected broken arm or doing a series of complex CT scans on a little girl's chest and stomach, the skill of working out how best to approach this small person is exactly the same.

'You've got to look them in the eye, and observe how they are with mum and dad. Then you decide if it's time to play the ogre or if it's time to be super kind.' The clues are there to be spotted. If mum or dad jump in when Martin asks their child a question, then it shows mum or dad, for whatever reason, is feeling protective. And designer labels head to foot on a two-year-old aren't *always* a sign of a spoilt nipper, but are more often than not.

'They're dead nosy, kids. Always listening to adults' conversation. If I've got a little rascal who just won't lie still, I might as a last resort try the loud whisper to mum, "Well, if he's not lying still I'm going to have to take him upstairs, give him an injection to put him to sleep, X-ray him and, of course, he'll need to stay in overnight." It's amazing how often that works. If it ever gets to brute force and ignorance – which is very rare indeed – I feel I've failed.' ∎

Guide to the X-ray Department

Today there are a wide variety of techniques for investigating a child for diseases, without resorting to surgery.

X-rays

The most common investigation, mainly used to look for broken bones, and chest complaints.

X-rays can be used to produce medical images as some parts of the body, e.g. bones, are not as transparent to X-rays as surrounding soft tissue. In radiography the beam of X-rays is passed through the patient and on to a photographic film to produce an image.

Ultrasound

A technique whereby high-frequency sounds are passed through the body's tissues. These interact with the tissues and reflect back to produce a picture. Most parts of the body can be imaged using ultrasound, and it is particularly good for looking at lumps in the abdomen and at the kidneys and bladder.

CT Scans

CT stands for 'Computerised Tomography'. It is the technique for imaging layers of the head and body using a computer to obtain very detailed cross-sectional images.

Nuclear Medicine

A technique whereby radioactive material is injected into parts of the body and then detailed photographs are taken by a 'gamma camera'. The photos can be used to obtain information about the functioning parts of the body, or to examine fractures which are unclear on X-rays.

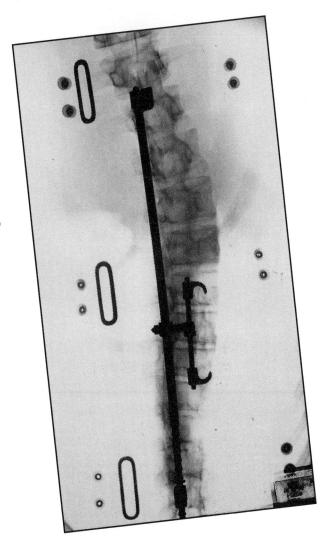

X-ray of a sixteen-year-old with Scoliosis (sideways curvature of the spine). A Harrington rod has been inserted to support and straighten the spine.

Stephen Penny
Senior Scientist

Stephen Penny is a senior scientist working in the hospital laboratories. A man of definite character and indeterminate age, he admits to arriving at the hospital in the early 1960s. This was a time when you had to wear evening dress at the annual hospital ball and junior staff were beginning a rebellious addiction to the Beatles.

Profile • Profile

When you think of a hospital, too often people forget the work of the labs. Stephen is one of fifty-eight laboratory staff who play a critical role in the treatment of the children. Modern medicine, quite simply, could not function without them. Whether it's providing evidence for diagnosing a tumour, tracking down a virus that is responsible for a dozen youngsters being on Ward 4, or assessing just how badly the kidneys of a baby on Intensive Care are working – the findings of the labs regularly decide the future of a child.

Not surprisingly, the work is rigorous and highly demanding. But Stephen's talents are not restricted to the labs alone. He has just earned his Gold Badge from the Transfusion Service, a reward for having donated more than fifty pints of his relatively rare blood. A keen local historian, he's also the consultant specialist (unpaid) in hospital anecdotes. The first of his offbeat SCH tales, Penny Pieces, appears opposite. ■

Penny Piece: The Strangest X-ray

Mummy was very old and rather stiff. It was nearly thirty years since she had last been X-rayed. She was carefully placed on a special trolley and wheeled to the door of her room so that the attendants might take her for her appointment.

Because Mummy was so old, Alison, who looked after her most, helped to move her for her X-ray. Several X-ray plates were made of Mummy from head to toe, and the films were pasted up on a large viewing box. Dr Alan Sprigg, Consultant Radiologist, came down to see the films. The only thing he could find wrong with her was a bad tooth. So Mummy went back to the comfort of her room, and Alison wondered what she might do next for Mummy.

Alan was asked if he might allow the wizard Martin to take Mummy through his CT scanner [see page 53]. A few days later Mummy set off to see Martin. This time it was raining and Alison made Mummy a special waterproof coat.

Alan watched Martin's screen with great interest and told Alison what he could see. This time Mummy's head showed really well; even her eyes could be seen. Mummy's favourite wooden box, which she had taken into the scanner with her, showed up well too. Alison was delighted.

The X-ray Department at the hospital had notched up a first. It was the first time that a mummy had been for a scan in the Children's Hospital. There was one more surprise. Mummy had not been a mother, but a girl of about fourteen! The Mummy lives in Sheffield City Museum in Weston Park, opposite the hospital. She came from Egypt; has never been unwrapped; has always been in her beautifully decorated case; and is about 3000 years old! Copies of her X-rays and her scans are displayed near her, with descriptions of what they show. Alison is Conservator in the Museum. Meanwhile, Gillian, the receptionist in X-ray, could not file the Mummy's details in the computer; it would not accept an age of more than 101 years!

Tricia Brennan
Accident and Emergency Consultant

There's no telling from one minute to the next what's going to happen in the department that Dr Tricia Brennan runs. One in four of Sheffield's children come through her doors. Some walk in, some come crying in their parents' arms, a few come in on a stretcher. In Accident and Emergency, consultant Tricia Brennan sees it all.

Profile • Profile •

Open twenty-four hours a day, seven days a week, the A & E Department is the hospital's window on the world. That means medical cover has to be available round the clock. Although she works part time, Dr Brennan is always on call. She has to divide her life between the demands of her four children, aged 13–19, 'all of whom are bigger than me', and the pressures of Casualty. Sometimes the two coincide. As the mother of a large family, she is no stranger to her department as a parent.

She trained at the Children's Hospital before moving on for more training in childhood trauma and dealing with child abuse. Now she's back. She prefers treating youngsters to adults in A & E 'because I like the way when they get better they are up and about rather than grumbling about the food'. But inevitably there are tragedies from time to time. Luckily her husband is a doctor so she gets plenty of support. 'I don't want him to do anything, I just want him to listen,' she says, 'because I know he'll understand.'

Drawing by Chloe Charlesworth Age 6

• Profile • Profile

This boy got hurt on the road by a car but the hospital helped me.
This is me now.

I ♥ the hospical

I was not looking Were I was going

Drawing by Cheryl Wilson Age 9

Every week Tricia Brennan holds a burns and trapped fingers clinic: these are the two most common accidents that occur in the home. She follows-up patients and tries to teach parents to stop the accidents happening again: 'It's difficult for parents to keep an eye on their children all the time, but once they have been in the wars usually both the children and their parents learn from their mistakes.'

But with 500 new cases coming through the doors each week, there's little chance of work drying up. ∎

Accident & Emergency

- The children's A & E Department is one of only four of its kind in England.
- All staff have specialised paediatric training, and the back-up of all the hospital's expertise.
- Some 40 000 'patient episodes' come through each year, which is 26 000 new patients.
- One in four children in Sheffield will come to A & E at some point in their lives.
- Some 70 per cent of children come in with 'trauma' – injuries from accidents at home, on the streets or at school.
- The rest are a mixed bag – from crying babies and minor infections, to a severe emergency such as a collapsed child.
- The department is focused around children: the decor smacks more of a nursery than a hospital, and the play facilities help dissipate anxiety, fear and boredom.
- Children are not little adults but growing and developing people. Their age and stage of development – physical, psychological and emotional – is taken into account.

Accident Prevention in the Home

Children under the age of five stand a greater risk of having an accident than any other age group. Some 550 000 are injured and 200 die every year. Many of these accidents could be prevented by simple safety precautions and thinking ahead. All children love to play and it is an essential part of their development, but some things are dangerous and it is important for parents to choose the right toys and place for play. One way of preventing accidents is to get into the habit of doing things in the safe way right from the beginning. Here are some simple steps you can take to make your home a safer place for your child.

Tips on How to Avoid Accidents at Home

Swallowing inedible items
- Lock your medicine cabinet.
- Safely store household substances out of reach.

Falls
- Install stair gates at the top and bottom of staircases.
- Never leave chairs or tables near to windows so that children can climb out.
- Never let tablecloths trail so that children can pull things off.

Scalds
- Use a stove guard.
- Put a thermostat on your hot-water tanks.
- Use a kettle with a curly lead.
- Use a kettle guard which secures it out of reach.
- Keep toys out of the kitchen so that you don't trip over them while carrying trays and hot pans.

Fires
- Don't let children play with matches or lighters.
- Install smoke detectors in the home.

Drownings
- Don't have garden ponds – fill them in and use as sandpits.
- Use slip-resistant bath mats in baths.

Glass lacerations
- Put unbreakable glass in doors or, alternatively, cover glass doors, table-tops and shower screens with inexpensive, easy-to-apply safety film for glass.

Hand burns
- Use fireguards.
- Put a guard around a glass-fronted oven.
- Keep irons out of reach.

•Children's Stories•

Accidents hurt . . .

I came to the Children's Hospital because I got a pain in my left leg. I like coming to the hospital because I like doing pictures all the time I come. I always like it but I don't like it when I have a blood test.

Adam Norie Age 10

I came to this hospital because I trapped my finger under a log at school. The doctors and nurses have been very kind and helpful to me. I have never had to wait long the three times I have been.

Gary Sheeran Age 11

Drawing by Emma Vickers Age 12

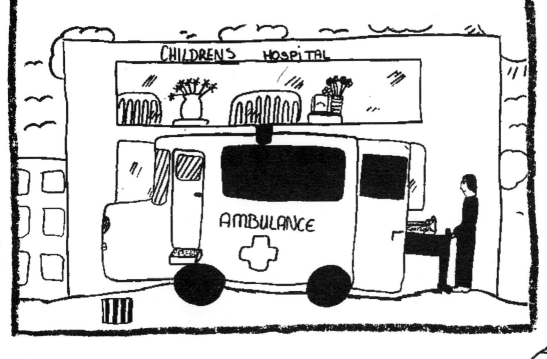

•Children's Stories•

. . . but the pain goes away.

When I was on holiday I fell down and hurt my arm. I went to the doctor's in Scotland and he said, if it wasn't getting better I must go to the hospital when I got home. I came to the Children's Hospital. I had an X-ray and had to sit very still while they took the picture of my bones. When the doctor showed me the X-ray picture she told my mummy
I had a broken arm. I had to have a pot on. The pot was very warm when they put it on. I had to keep the pot on for a long time to make it better

Fiona Age 6

this docter is going to help some one.

Drawing by Ryan Wilson

The Four Seasons

The changing seasons dramatically affect the sorts of problems that bring children into A & E.

Spring and Summer

As the weather improves and nights get lighter, sprains, fractures and lacerations are caused by outdoor play and sport.
Ingestions of plants, berries, fungi.
Burns and heat stroke from the sun.

Autumn

Fractures caused by falls from conker trees. Beginning of winter sports injuries, including burns and breaks from the dry ski slope.

Winter

Scalds from hot drinks, burns from fires, stoves and radiators.
Fractures from sledging, sliding, and winter sports.
Chest infections: bronchiolitis, pneumonia and asthma.

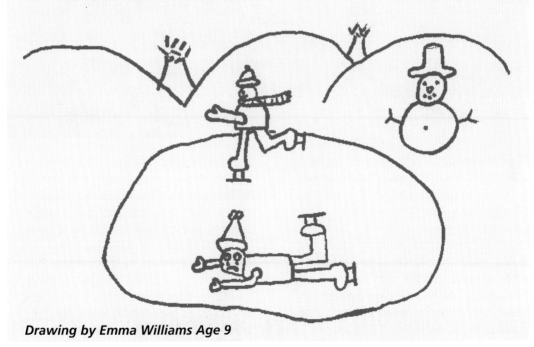

Drawing by Emma Williams Age 9

A & E: A Day <u>in the Life of</u> <u>Dr Anneka Woodmansey</u>

The day starts, as usual, with paper-work. There is a pile of computer mail to go to GPs which needs to be read through because occasionally the computer generates nonsense.

There are also the results of blood tests, X-rays, etc. to be checked with the case notes to make sure the right diagnosis has been made, and I contact a couple of patients who need further treatment or to come in for review.

I then join a few colleagues seeing patients. My first one is a little girl who has refused to use her arm ever since her father pulled her up by the hands and thought he heard something click. The story is typical of a pulled elbow where one of the forearm bones (the radius) is pulled from its supporting ligament near the elbow. Fortunately, a relatively simple manipulation usually restores everything to normal, and after a quick twist (and a few indignant tears) the little girl trots off to the playroom and has soon forgotten all about it.

Next there is a phone call from a mum wanting some advice about her child who has sprayed deodorant in his face and mouth. I ask her to bring him in so we can assess whether he has inhaled any.

The next patient is a toddler who has eaten some berries from the garden. Her mum brought along some of the berries and a branch of the bush, but we cannot match it up with anything in our books. I contact a member of the University's Botany Department who identifies it as a non-toxic shrub, and so the child goes home.

Another phone call, this time about a poorly baby whose mum has called her GP but is still worried. And I see several patients returning for review – cuts, an infected finger, a boil and a chesty baby.

Meanwhile a colleague is seeing a two-year-old who has managed to get a brass plant pot stuck on his head. Several attempts at removal with Vaseline, soap, and cold water are unsuccessful, by which time the boy is getting distressed and his scalp is becoming swollen inside the pot. Eventually the fire brigade are called in the hope that they can use their metal cutters, and we give the boy some sedation in preparation. The firemen end up using hydraulic jacks mounted on a doorframe to compress the top of the pot and widen the opening, finally releasing the boy after a two-hour ordeal.

My last two patients have both fallen and cut their faces. They have cuts which are in awkward places but a dexterous nurse makes a good job of both.

My shift has now finished and the department is quiet, so I am able to leave on time. It's been another interesting day.

Substances Swallowed by Sheffield Children

In the Accident and Emergency waiting-room are two boxes. Their contents are a warning to all parents of small children. They contain substances that have been swallowed and objects that have been retrieved from the stomachs of Sheffield children.

They include:

Jeyes disinfectant	Worming pills
Bleach	for dogs
Wallpaper strippers	Batteries
Nail polish	Coins
Nail polish remover	Clock winding
Leather dye (black)	key
Antiseptic	Holly berries
Laxatives	End of glass
Paracetamol/aspirins	thermometer
Floor cleaner	Earrings
Travel sickness pills	Plastic toys
Cough syrup	

The Hospital

1. The Roofhouse Playcentre – a play area for brothers and sisters of patients
2. Rooms for parents to stay overnight
3. Chrystal Radio and TV
4. Personnel, Administration and Finance
5. Ward 4: Medical ward
6. Ward 3: Oncology ward
7. Ward 7: Surgical ward
8. Ward 8: Day care
9. Ward 9: General medical/renal problems
10. Junior doctors' mess and rooms to sleep when on call
11. Chief Executive's and Director of Nursing's offices

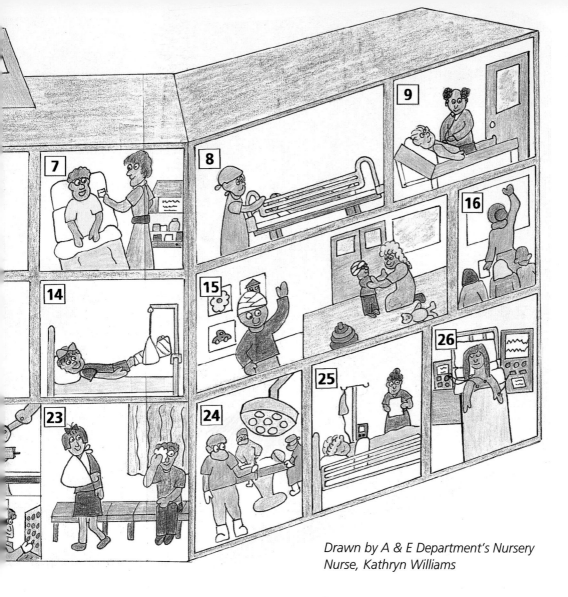

Drawn by A & E Department's Nursery Nurse, Kathryn Williams

12 Ward 2: Medical and some day care
13 Ward 1: Neonatal intensive care
14 Ward 5: Orthopaedics
15 Ward 6: Ear, nose and throat, and plastic surgery
16 Lecture theatres
17 Coffee lounge for staff and parents
18 Dining-room and kitchen
19 Reception and Out-patients

20 X-ray
21 Women's Royal Voluntary Service tea bar
22 Switchboard
23 Accident and Emergency
24 Operating theatres
25 Recovery
26 Intensive care unit

Profile ◆ Profile

Few practices in Britain can boast a specialist Children's Hospital on the doorstep. It's a bonus appreciated by the four partners at Park Health Centre. Between them they see 29 000 patients a year and make over 3000 home visits. Many of these involve small children. In 1992, nearly 200 children of the practice were admitted to the Children's Hospital.

For Dr Murton the hospital's presence is deeply reassuring. 'It's just knowing they're there. If you have any queries you can ring. They're always willing to see children and never say, "Don't be silly, don't bother us."'

Orthopaedic cases, ear, nose and throat problems, and skin conditions like eczema form the bulk of the cases sent up to the Children's. Add to that the seasonal chest infections, the broken bones in the light summer evenings, and the common surgical procedures: the appendicectomies, hernias and circumcisions.

There are the less common causes for referral, too: the two children in the practice on growth hormone, or the child who drank an entire bottle of calamine lotion, for example. A recent visit to a boy with a fever and rash resulted in Dr Murton rushing him straight up to the hospital in his car. The boy had meningitis.

At times like this the Children's Hospital is invaluable. 'You've got to see things through a child's eyes.' Parents and his patients confirm his view. 'They say how attuned the staff are, how they understand the needs of sick children.' ∎

A GP's Practice

'A godsend' is how GP Dr Damien Murton describes the Children's Hospital. He and the team at Park Health Centre, Duke Street, Sheffield, should know. Their busy inner-city practice has 8000 people on its books, 1500 of whom are under sixteen. More than 500 are under five.

Primary Health Care

For over a century the standard of care at the Children's Hospital has been praised, but the overall improvement in health of the city's children owes as much to the work that goes on outside the hospital doors.

All over Sheffield, teams of GPs, health visitors, midwives, district nurses and others provide vital immunisations, with advice on how to prevent infectious disease and education for better baby and child care – primary health care.

Just over a hundred years ago, for every 1000 children born in Sheffield, 169 died. Infectious disease, poor housing and sanitation accounted for most of this.

At the turn of the century came some far-reaching developments.

- 1899 Two women inspectors (or health visitors) were appointed, qualified as nurses, midwives and sanitary inspectors. They gave advice on food, baby care and pregnancy.

- 1905 A School Medical Officer was appointed, and recommended the medical inspection of school children.

- 1907 The first baby consultations were held in Sheffield. Just one parent and child attended. Within ten years, attendance rose to 33 000.

- 1907 The first school meals for needy children.

Today, practices like Park Health Centre offer a range of baby clinics, antenatal classes and advice on parenthood. The government has set immunisation targets, but patients often place a low priority on preventive medicine, and childhood immunisation has proved a difficult concept to get across. A concerted effort by a team of midwives, health visitors and GPs has led to a high percentage uptake of baby immunisation. School-entry immunisation has proved more difficult.

Primary care at Park Health Centre is all about teamwork.

John Stent
Leading Ambulanceman

John Stent is 'right thankful' that he does not have to visit the Children's Hospital more frequently. He is a Leading Ambulanceman, a member of the South Yorkshire Metropolitan Ambulance and Paramedic Service.

'I'm not the sort of person who enjoys rushing out to an RTA [road traffic accident].' But when he has to, he takes a pride in tackling it professionally. John joined the service in 1968. Having nursed his mother for many years, he was initially drawn to nursing, but the pay was not enticing and John went 'on the buses' instead. In the end, the desire to help people in a rewarding job got the better of him.

As a Leading Ambulanceman, he is one of five who manage Middlewood Ambulance Station. The station has eighteen ambulances. Some are reserved for day transport, others for out-patients. The rest are for Accident and Emergency. In an emergency, the call comes through to control. Control decide which vehicle is closest. A quarter of a century in the service has taught John to be prepared for any eventuality. Some just ring screaming: '"Send me an ambulance!" You don't know what the problem is. Others just say, "There's been an accident at a junction." We have no idea how many are involved, how many are in the cars.'

Drawing by Anthony Hughes Age 12

The ambulance staff are required to make an instant assessment. 'If there are several casualties we have to make priorities. We may go for the quietest, because we know those screaming and shouting are not choking.' In accidents, children present particular problems. 'Often they can't tell you where the pain is. They thrash around. Getting through at a time like that is very difficult. You have to try to be the loving father figure to them.'

Although John and his team are called to attend children relatively infrequently, there are sad exceptions. All cot deaths are taken straight to the Children's Hospital.

It is a job few would envy. But the training John and his colleagues go through is intense. It has to be, given the amount of distress and trauma they see. 'As a professional you have to cut out. If you rush to someone with a chest pain, they are not in the slightest interested in the accident you have just attended.'

John has been doing the job so long there is not much that keeps him awake at night. 'And anyway, I'm usually too busy working.' ▨

Drawing by Rebecca Hardwick Age 7

South Yorkshire Metropolitan Ambulance and Paramedic Service

The service John Stent works for serves 1.3 million patients all over Barnsley, Doncaster, Rotherham and Sheffield. It works alongside thirty hospitals and treatment centres, one of which is the Children's Hospital. Over 600 staff and 207 ambulances cover an area of 600 square miles from thirteen ambulance stations. The Accident and Emergency ambulance crews respond to four sorts of calls:

- 999 emergency calls;
- urgent hospital admissions, and transfers requested by doctors (such as the Children's 'flying baby' service);
- major incidents and civil disturbances;
- calls to safeguard other emergency services.

Drawing by Wayne Boot Age 5

Penny Piece: Time to Reflect

The Accident and Emergency Department at the hospital has a foyer with chairs, tables, toys and games. It was not so in the old Casualty Department. Patients used to have to wait in the corridor. As more and more patients attended Casualty an extension became necessary. The old place was demolished, and a new building rose in its place. Casualty became Accident and Emergency, and new surgical wards were opened above the new department.

Then, as now, this department was open twenty-four hours a day, seven days a week. It was extensively re-equipped, with the latest modern technology. The Consultant Doctor in charge was Mrs Cynthia Illingworth. When she retired, staff and friends gathered in the dining-room to wish her well. In her speech she reviewed the old days in Casualty, and contrasted them with the modern A & E Department. How glad she was to have high-tech aids, more space, better working conditions. These were marvellous improvements. But the best piece of equipment, she said, did not cost much at all. It was the distorting mirror.

Nearly every child stops in front of it and sometimes even adults take a look. Usually there are shrieks of laughter.

Less is More
Arthur Kaufman, Clinical Psychologist advises

Do you automatically feel sorry for all children in hospital? Well, don't, as this may do them little good when all is said and done.

If a child is seriously ill or injured and likely to remain so, that is one thing.

However, if the illness or injury is short-lived or not particularly serious, try not to go overboard with lavish gifts or too much attention as, firstly, it does not take most children very long to realise they are on to a good thing nor, secondly, does it need much imagination or effort on their part to exploit the situation.

The situation can even become 'hyper-exploitable' if, say, the parents are separated or divorced and happen to be active competitors in the 'Please love Mummy/Daddy the most' stakes, with all the proceeds going to Little Darling Number One peering out from behind mountains of expensive presents and video-games.

Even in the case of a sudden accident or acute illness, where a child may be hospitalised for only a short period, there is a risk of spoiling him or her for years to come.

Many children are very clever at picking up signs of over-concern on the part of worried parents. Moreover, parents tend to feel guilty because, 'if only' they had done something different, little Johnny or lovely Suzy would never have landed in hospital in the first place.

Feeling guilt in such circumstances is, of course, a normal reaction. However, it is important that the child does not become aware of this, since it can be used as a way of manipulating anxious parents or other relatives by most unfair means. Some children are particularly effective at not only 'turning on' the tears but also in using guilt-inducing phrases and gestures capable of melting the sternest of grown-up hearts.

While all children need that extra bit of attention and fussing over when recovering in hospital, it is important that this be carried out in a sensible and 'measured' way rather than overdone at the parents' future emotional and psychological expense.

In the end, it is usually good old mum or dad who will have to cope with the long-term consequences of unnecessary indulgence during what may have been a difficult time for any conscientious parent. Resisting the urge to give in to children by giving too much too easily is sensible advice to keep in mind.

School's Out

for Arthur Kaufman, Clinical Psychologist

Each year I think of leaving town when July comes round. That's when many children come home with school reports which leave a lot to be desired. Most parents make a little bit of a fuss over the results but soon remember that in their day they were no better themselves. However, some parents take a different line.

I recall a case of a ten-year-old called Neil, whose over-anxious and over-intellectual parents hit the roof after reading a whole battery of comments in the vein of 'could do better – doesn't concentrate – day-dreams all day' from a host of frustrated teachers.

Neil was promptly marched down for a 'cure' to his unsuspecting family doctor who, after hearing the sorry tale, cleverly decided to pass the buck in my direction.

When he was dragged into my office I had never seen such a cleanly scrubbed child. What's more, his parents brought with them a very large folder containing all his work books since the time he started school, and a large quantity of carefully word-processed information besides.

Having been through this sort of thing all too often, I pretended to thumb through the documentation and then got on with examining Neil's intelligence. As predicted, he turned out to be on the higher side of average and I was able to reassure his parents that they had bequeathed to young Master the best their genes had to offer.

I then explained to Neil on his own that it would be nice if he could manage to move up a place or two in his class rankings instead of remaining too near the bottom of the form, which would then get his parents off his back (and they off mine). This relieved his worries about having to be a super-scholar, which he wasn't cut out to be in the first place.

After a further word with the parents, Dad admitted he was nearly thrown out of two schools before deciding to knuckle down to some work and Mum blurted out she still couldn't spell properly to save her life. The consultation ended with Dad looking a bit choked and Mum holding a tissue to her nose – in other words, a success.

I often wonder how all the Neils I've seen eventually turn out. Do they go on to brilliant careers or do they fall away in the frantic race for money and status? Perhaps in my declining years I'll come across some of them who will tell me how terrible it was until they came my way, or how catastrophic things were after I had 'interfered' with their lives.

In the meantime, I've definitely booked this year's holiday for July and I am beginning to feel tons better already.

Profile • Profile

What do the teachers have to say about their work at SCH?

Michael Ibbertson and Lorraine Cooper teach on Ward 3, the Oncology Ward.

'Our job on Ward 3 includes the skills of a traditional teacher and more. We teach the National Curriculum and keep in touch with each child's school, but we also aim to provide sympathetic guidance as they learn. If parents or children wish to share a problem or worry, we're always ready to listen. We may not have the answers, but so often it helps to talk things over and there've been many times that we've been able to comfort in some way.

'Inevitably, we have our sad times on Ward 3, but there is also a cheerfulness and warmth – and not just from the cooker as we take out our seventh or eighth tray of biscuits on Baking Day! There's the joy of one of our little ones discovering the fun of working on the computer for the first time, or the excitement of the fancy dress party at Christmas.

'It's an old saying, but we feel we really do learn a lot from our pupils and their families, coping as they are with the trauma of very serious illness. We consider it a real privilege to be a small part of the very special world of Ward 3.' ■

Drawing by Sarah Booth

Teachers

Just because children are in hospital, it doesn't mean they can bunk off school! Provided the children are well enough, those in for five days or more are taught by one of the eight teachers in the hospital. They aim to keep children up to date with schoolwork and to give them a normal daily routine. Some children have even taken GCSEs while strung up in traction. Nor does the teaching end there – if children are recovering at home, they can have home tutors.

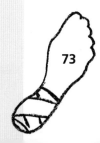

Pharmacy

Ask anyone about the pharmacy services in a hospital, and most will respond with a blank stare and perhaps imagine a sort of chemist's somewhere inside the building.

In fact, the Pharmacy provides a full range of drugs to treat both in-patients and out-patients, anything from routine inhalers for asthma to highly toxic compounds, especially made up, to attack certain types of cancer.

The day starts early. Between 7.00 and 7.30 a.m. the porters collect the empty drug boxes from all the wards. The pharmacy technicians operate a 'top-up' service for each ward after agreeing a stocklist of regularly used drugs with the sister in charge. Nurses do not have to worry about re-ordering that way; they are free to spend more time with their patients.

Sometimes the technicians get special requests. Can they prepare a batch of anaesthetic ice lollipops for a child with an ulcerated mouth? Can they disguise a bitter drug as a chocolate drop?

The hospital is the regional centre for the treatment of childhood cancer, and the pharmacy specialises in making the toxic drugs for chemotherapy. The drugs themselves are dispensed using 'isolators' – a way of packaging the drugs and keeping them sterile which makes it much safer for doctors and nurses to handle them.

Basic Pharmacy Facts

- The Pharmacy purchases over £1 million pounds worth of drugs and supplies each year.
- Over 70 000 items are issued to in-patients and out-patients each year.
- A specialised dispensing unit produces about 2000 batches of TPN (total parental nutrition, or intravenous feeding) per year.
- About 2500 cytotoxic drug items (very toxic drugs often used in cancer treatment) are dispensed.
- Over 20 000 syringes are produced under sterile conditions for individual patients each year.
- About 2400 different types of drugs are used in the pharmacy.

Penny Piece: Off the Back of a Lorry

Sylvia and Susan (who work in Pathology) were sitting quietly in their office when there was a knock at the door. At this time they rarely opened the door because the excavators and lorries were making such a noise. Durham Road had once been a quiet residential street; then the hospital took over the houses one by one to accommodate its expanding services, and now the houses were being demolished for the multi-million-pound Phase I.

At the door stood a giant of a man; Susan's heart missed at least one beat, but he had such a nice smile, and he carefully wiped his feet when he came through the door. He drove a digger, and in his hands he had what looked like a lump of clay. What was it, he wanted to know? Sylvia and Susan looked surprised, but then carefully washed off some of the mud to reveal a stoneware jar. It looked really old, but it was glazed, so it couldn't be prehistoric! The driver was pleased to leave the jar with Susan, who took it to the Sheffield City Museum across the road from the hospital. There was no one in that day who could help; the pottery expert was on holiday.

'Mincemeat,' said someone. 'Jam,' said another. 'Beer,' said a third. 'Lemonade,' said someone in authority. Unfortunately, the digger driver had not found any stopper to the jar, and it was empty. Just then, Professor Emery ambled in. 'I know what that is.' (Of course.) 'It's a stoneware jar!' Sylvia and Susan laughed, but Prof. had not yet finished. 'In the *old* days,' (here we go), 'Laboratory chemicals used to be brought from the suppliers to the hospital in these jars, and they used to go back to be refilled. Obviously, this one fell off the back of the lorry!'

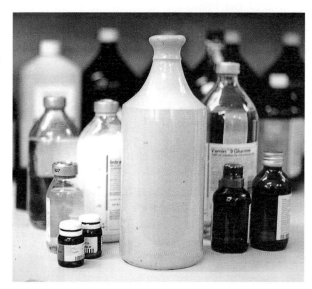

If you ask nicely in Pharmacy you may be allowed to see this small piece of hospital history. It is not a fake, it is the genuine thing!

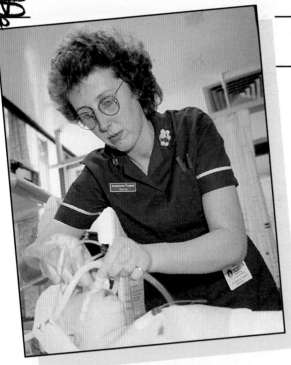

Anne-Marie Rogers
Sister on Paediatric
Intensive Care Unit

It takes an unusual person to want to work in the highly stressful atmosphere of a paediatric intensive care unit. Anne-Marie Rogers fits the bill: a keen traveller and rider of British motorbikes, she has also tried her hand at judo and parachuting . Her working life began as a fork-lift truck driver in Solihull, but when 5000 pairs of socks crashed to the ground Anne-Marie knew her vocation lay elsewhere.

Profile • Profile •

By a route that took her through nursing training in Oxford, fruit-picking on a kibbutz, work in a nursing home and then intensive care units in Hereford and Jerusalem, she arrived in Sheffield. It turned out to be work well-suited to a woman who thrives on the unpredictable, who describes herself as 'a doer rather than a thinker'.

Many of the children are critically ill when they arrive in intensive care. 'We get to the children through the parents. They tell us so much. And we put photos on the beds. When the kids come round it's amazing how we feel we know them.'

With the high quality of dedicated specialist care on ICU, most children leave the unit well. But tragically, a few do not. At these times, all nurses have their own way of coping. 'Mine is to get out for a long walk with the dog,' says Anne-Marie. 'As we walk I think it all through – what I have done and what I should have done. I know if I didn't have the dog I'd sit and stew.'

Intensive care treatment is expensive. Almost £20 000-worth of monitors and ventilators surrounds each bed. As the biggest paediatric intensive care unit in the

Sister Anne-Marie by Matthew Jackson

area, there is frequently pressure on the four beds for which the unit is funded and staffed. An outbreak of croup or bronchiolitis can push numbers over the limit to six, even seven children. At such times the nursing staff are stretched almost to breaking-point. Not infrequently, hospitals with critically ill children requiring intensive care have to ring from hospital to hospital, even town to town, in search of an ICU bed.

Despite the sad times, the unit remains a bright, hopeful place, and Anne-Marie and her dedicated colleagues stay cheerful: 'You hang on to the hope there's a chance for every child. You have to believe it. Or you'd go home thinking you'd failed.' ■

Throughout Britain there are neonatal intensive care units, widely known as SCBUs (Special Care Baby Units). These units manage critically ill newborn babies, many of whom have been born prematurely. There are only twenty major specialised units for critically ill children and infants in Britain. Sheffield has the unit for the Trent Region. A paediatric ICU provides for the specialised needs of the critically ill child, and is staffed by paediatricians, paediatric anaesthetists and children's nurses, all experienced and trained in paediatric intensive care.

One Year in the Life of the Intensive Care Unit (1992)

Children admitted to Sheffield Children's Hospital Intensive Care Unit: 213

From Sheffield, 109, the rest from all over South Yorkshire and beyond.

Seasonal respiratory problems (e.g., croup, bronchiolitis, epiglottitis): 28 per cent.

Other non-surgical emergencies (e.g., drowning, asthma, meningitis, inhalation of foreign bodies): 28 per cent

Emergency surgery (e.g., lacerated spleen): 16 per cent.

Elective surgery (e.g., spinal fusion, major orthopaedic surgery or ear, nose and throat): 10 per cent.

Trauma cases (result of accidents): 8 per cent.

Flying Babies

The Intensive Care Unit offers a highly specialised service for children, which acts as a magnet for referrals from a wide area. In particular,' the Unit offers a retrieval service for very sick babies: sending out its own team of doctors and nurses to any hospital where there is a child in trouble, to bring them back to the safety of the Children's ICU. This is the story of one such retrieval.

2 p.m. A cold January afternoon in Intensive Care. Sister Anne-Marie Rogers glances round the Unit at her four small patients, their monitors bleeping regularly. The phone rings.

2.10 p.m. A five-week-old baby is having severe breathing problems at Mansfield Hospital, where there's no paediatric ICU. Now Mansfield want to transfer her to the Children's. Anne-Marie bleeps Dr Teresa Dorman, Consultant Anaesthetist; instructs Sister Jane Walker to prepare ventilating equipment and drugs; and phones for an ambulance.

2.15 p.m. Teresa Dorman is on to Mansfield Hospital to find out more about the child's condition. The Operating Department Assistant packs the incubator with heart and blood pressure monitors.

2.30 p.m. The ambulance arrives and is loaded up. Siren on, blue lights flashing, it roars off towards Mansfield, thirty miles away. Strapped in the back are Jane, Teresa and the ODA (a technician who specialises in ventilating equipment). They are quiet,

concentrating on the task ahead.

3.10 p.m. The ambulance arrives. Teresa, Jane and the ODA run on ahead. The ambulancemen follow with the incubator.

3.15 p.m. The team burst into the Children's Ward. Teresa quickly and calmly takes control. One of the baby's lungs has collapsed, and she needs more and more oxygen. Her temperature has dropped rapidly. Examining the baby, Teresa decides to try using a slightly larger tube to carry the oxygen into the baby's chest. 'Get me a 3. It's larger and might get more oxygen into the baby.' Teresa takes over the ventilating of the baby, rhythmically squeezing the rubber bag full of oxygen connected to the baby's tube in order to regulate the baby's breathing. The baby is wrapped in a small, shiny, metallic survival blanket to help raise her temperature.

3.18 p.m. Jane attaches an oxygen saturation monitor to the baby's toe, and Teresa sets up two drips, morphine and glucose, into tiny veins on the baby's foot and hand. The baby's heartbeat can be seen as pulses on the portable monitor.

3.25 p.m. As the baby is sedated by the morphine, Teresa concentrates on changing the breathing tube into the lungs, delicately manoeuvring the new tube down the baby's nose.

3.35 p.m. The baby begins to stabilise.

3.50 p.m. Teresa judges the baby is stable enough to attempt the journey to the

Children's. It is a delicate decision: the baby needs to get back to the full support of ICU as soon as possible, but the journey could trigger a change in her condition.

The baby is put into the incubator and wheeled to the ambulance.

4.00 p.m. The ambulance sets off at a steady speed. It is a nail-biting time. Teresa keeps a watchful eye on the monitors and continues to squeeze the bag, doing the baby's breathing for it. Back in ICU, a team stand by.

4.50 p.m. Relief as the ambulance arrives back at the hospital, and ICU. After the baby is stabilised, her anxious parents, who have just arrived, are reunited with their precious daughter.

6.30 p.m. Having talked to Mr and Mrs Colclough and handed over to the night-time anaesthetist, Dr Teresa Dorman shrugs on her coat and heads home into the dark, wintry night. Another good job well done, another 'life saved'. In fact, just another day at the Children's.

Samantha Colclough was suffering from bronchiolitis, pneumonia and a collapsed lung. After nine days on ICU, she was able to go to a normal medical ward to complete her recovery. She is now completely well and at home.

•Children's Stories•

Samantha Colclough's Story

Samantha's mum picks up the story after her baby's arrival on ICU.

It was very hard and upsetting to see our baby with tubes and wires attached to her body; she looked just like a lifeless doll. I couldn't believe she was my baby and the crying I was doing just wouldn't stop. The doctor said to touch and talk to her but I found this very difficult. I loved her very much and to do this and love her more, with the possibility she might not make it, was torment in itself. During this time, we were encouraged to care for her, clean her eyes and change her nappy which I felt I needed to do so she still felt as if she was my baby.

One morning when we came down, she was awake. She could cry but couldn't make any noise and she looked so pitiful as she couldn't understand what was happening; her face kept going red and tears welled up but no noise would come, and this was very upsetting. There was also the day, two weeks later, that I was finally allowed to hold her again. The joy I felt was just like when she was born and I was given her to hold for the first time.

After six days the ventilator was half taken out and was just in her nose. When she cried this time the noise could come again, and I said I didn't mind how much she cried in the future as long as she was all right. On the eighth day they took the tube out altogether and just put an oxygen box over her head. During the day she didn't seem to be doing very well and they said it might have to go back in again, but that evening she seemed to say 'no way' and just came on leaps and bounds. The next morning we were transferred on to a ward.

The anxiety and stress we were under was not something I would wish to repeat or for any other parent to have to experience. But the care and attention that both Samantha and ourselves received in the ICU was marvellous. And I should like to praise the staff and thank them for returning our baby back to us alive and well.

•Children's Stories•

Luke's Story

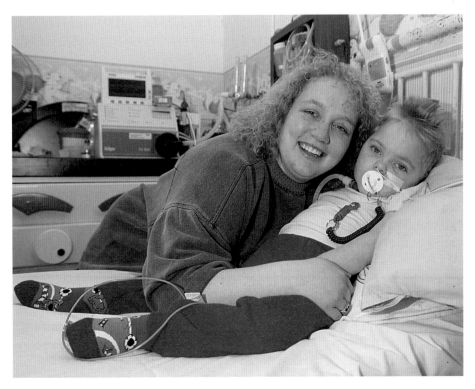

Earlier this year, one Sunday morning in Recovery, the hospital held a party. It was a 'goodbye party' for a rather special patient. As such it marked a milestone in his recovery. Some two years and three months earlier he had been rushed into ICU. Barring a few hours' visit to the hospital canteen in his specially adapted wheelchair, he had spent every night of those last twenty-seven months in Intensive Care. If it were not for the sheer determination of his parents and the support of the hospital, he would still be there now.

(continued on next page)

(Luke's Story continued)

Aged six months, Luke Jackson had been brought into the Children's ICU with symptoms like pneumonia. When the time came to ween him off the ventilator, his consultant Jerry Wales noticed he was not moving his arms and legs properly. Dr Wales asked for a special scan. The scan told him that Luke had an inflammatory infection of the spine, diagnosed as Transverse Myelitis – a very rare condition. A virus had attacked his spine and was spreading. Soon it was to rob Luke of the use of his arms and legs.

To this day the only movements Luke can make are with his head and his lips. He has the distinction of being the youngest child documented suffering from the disease. There is no chance of him recovering from his paralysis. His breathing will be done for him by a machine for the rest of his life.

The bleak outlook did not stop Claire and Dale Jackson from continuing the fight – not just to will Luke to live, but to get him home and to get the council to find the money to adapt the house for Luke to live in. Room was needed for special equipment and bathing facilities, ramps for his wheelchair, accommodation for his carers. There were times in hospital when Claire and Dale could not imagine Luke getting through the day – let alone getting him home to join his twin brother Adam and elder brother Matt.

These obstacles have been overcome but life with Luke is still very much based on trial and error. He has broken ground again – he is the youngest ever patient in Britain to be ventilated at home. A team of six carers – all given a crash course by the hospital ICU – provide Luke with the twenty-four-hour attention he needs. Part of the house has been turned into a miniature ICU complete with bleeps, wires and tubes. Claire and Dale could probably teach the next batch of student nurses all they need to know about the care of ventilated babies.

But the advantages of home life are clear. Mum and Dad don't have to spend hours every day away from home. Adam and Matt don't have to be dragged along to hospital. And most important of all, Luke's personality is coming on leaps and bounds. Claire and Dale are wholly in charge now – just like other parents. They are doing what they think is best for their son, dividing their time more equally among their children.

The hospital has not forgotten them. Claire and Dale both know the hospital's staff are just a phonecall away – if need be. As someone said at the party in Recovery – it has taken a couple of years longer than anyone thought to get Luke home, but better late than never.

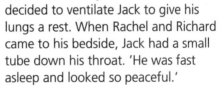

•Children's Stories•

A Momentary Crisis

It was Boxing Day at the O'Malley household. Rachel and Richard were holding a party for the family. Little Jack, their cheery, robust, eight-month-old son had been put to bed. Out of the blue he developed a strange cough. 'It was a strange sound,' said Richard, 'a bit like the way a dog sometimes sneezes.'

It turned out that Jack had bronchiolitis. Three days after Christmas, Richard remembers, 'Jack was fighting that hard to breathe I was worried his heart would stop.' The doctors decided to move Jack to Intensive Care. 'You think the worst in Intensive Care. I kept looking for reassurance from everyone.' The anaesthetists

decided to ventilate Jack to give his lungs a rest. When Rachel and Richard came to his bedside, Jack had a small tube down his throat. 'He was fast asleep and looked so peaceful.'

For the next two days the O'Malleys' hopes of a quick recovery were raised then dashed. Jack developed a chest infection and then pneumonia. As 1992 became 1993, Rachel and Richard were by his bedside. Then Jack slowly turned the corner.

Sixteen days after he had first arrived Jack was taken off the ventilator. He had made a complete recovery. 'The day they took if all off,' remembers Richard, 'it was like we had got our child back. With all the tubes and leads, he'd been unrecognisable. It was brilliant to see. It had all happened in three weeks, but it felt like three years.'

Joan Patterson
Intensive Care Nurse

Joan Patterson, a local lass, came to the Children's Hospital in 1976 to train. She has never left and is now an enrolled nurse on Intensive Care.

Profile • Profile

'**A**s a child I thought nursing was a glorious profession,' remembers Joan. 'I'd look at all those pictures in magazines. It seemed like a fairy tale.' Does nursing live up to Joan's expectations? 'There are occasionally days when I can't wait to get home and put my feet up, but those are usually when it is terribly quiet.' When it is busy, Joan is happy. 'Then there is a buzz about the work. You are more alert. You're on your toes.'

Intensive Care is a part of the hospital that fills many nurses with anxiety. Not Joan: 'I like to have a patient to look after. To really get in there and to work 100 per cent.'

There remains a good deal to keep a smile on Joan's face: 'An absolute no-hoper who makes it through. Telling a doctor something you've noticed and being taken seriously. Striking up a special relationship with a parent.'

Nurses in ICU cannot have a phobia about new technology. Some £20 000-worth of it surrounds each Intensive Care bed. Joan is philosophical: 'The technology is here to stay. Me, I'm Mrs Practical – and you get used to it.'

On the Unit the most knife-edge incidents are almost daily occurrences. 'Say a baby of a few weeks old comes in with bronchiolitis whose oxygen saturation or heart-rate drops and you have to hand bag him [ventilate by hand]. It's dramatic but, in a strange way, for us it is almost run of the mill.' ∎

Twenty Years On
Sandra Sargeant, Nursing Sister

Russell Hallowes was just four when, playing with matches, he set fire to polystyrene ceiling tiles at home. The molten tiles dropped over him and his younger brother Kevin. Russell received horrific 90 per cent burns.

Sandra Sargeant, then the Sister on the Burns and Plastics Ward, remembers the incident well. It was February, 1972, and she had just returned from her honeymoon.

The burns on Russell's face, arms and trunk were severe. Smoke had damaged his throat and lungs, and for years he needed a tracheostomy. 'It was a miracle that he lived,' remembers Sandra. 'I'm sure it was his determination that brought him through.'

Both Russell and his brother survived. Nursing Russell back to health was a long, painful process. His dressings took nearly two hours to change: left on for three days to allow the skin to heal, they would then have to be soaked off in a saline bath. 'I can't ever remember Russell complaining. I think it was a case of big boys don't cry. But you could see the beads of sweat on his brow, so he was obviously in pain.'

As Russell got better, he was left with contractures (tight tissue) in his arms and elbows. His surgeon, Mr Miller, had to perform countless skin grafts. So badly had Russell been burnt that it was hard to find skin to graft.

Through it all his parents Brian, a miner, and Clare pulled together and Auntie Celia was around to provide support. Sandra nursed him on and off until he was fourteen. Later, he moved to an adult hospital for treatment, but never forgot to pop in to see Sandra on the ward.

In time, Russell became a motor mechanic – even servicing the car of Mr Miller, his surgeon. Then, in the summer of 1992, Sandra received an invitation to a wedding. On 1 August 1992, at St James's Church, Woodhouse, Russell married Dawn. 'It was a very emotional day,' says Sandra.

The Porters

Not many staff have Dave Cox's (left) perspective on the hospital. When he was a toddler his father noticed that he was not crawling properly. A visit to his GP led to the Children's Hospital, where he was diagnosed with left hemiplegia – a condition which disables the whole of the left side of his body.

Fifteen years on Dave came back to hospital – this time as a porter. He has stayed ever since, working the last six years on nights. 'Despite being a patient at Ryegate, I was the only child who went to a normal school. I'm just very proud that I've been on both sides of the hospital.'

If the Disablement Resettlement Officer had had her way, it would never have happened. When Dave told her he wanted to be a hospital porter, she was adamant: 'Oh, that's not possible.'

The hospital at night is very different from the bustle of the day. Besides the obvious quiet and dark, Dave says the feeling among the porters is even more tight-knit. He and his partner, Phil Darlow, have routine duties – collecting laundry and refuse from all the wards, moving equipment – and they have to be on hand for any emergencies. A child might need admitting in the middle of the night to the wards. Thieves might be breaking into the junior doctors' mess. It has happened more than once in the last year.

Dave explains his partnership with Phil: 'I'm the brains, he's the brawn.' Phil, who has triumphed as the hospital Father Christmas for the last couple of years, does not disagree.

Dave was on the phone to the same Resettlement Officer only recently. 'Oh, really?' she said. 'Is that where you work? Well . . . we're not always right.' ∎

Works Departments usually only get the limelight when things go wrong, but without this group of people the building would grind to a halt. On a typical day, Clive could be repairing the hydro-therapy pool at Ryegate, unblocking a sink on the ward, fixing an earthing clamp to a bath in the nurses' home, or even glazing a new set of hospital windows. The department is twenty men strong – plumbers, electricians, fitters, joiners – all keeping the fabric of the place in good repair.

Clive reckons the time the hospital appreciated them most was one September morning in 1991. He and a mate were working in the basement area next to Theatre when they noticed water dripping down from the ceiling – which was the Theatre floor. Half an hour later, Clive and most of the department were shoulder to shoulder with consultants and nurses, passing buckets, in two to three feet of cold water.

Apart from his skill as a plumber, Clive has talents in clinic. He tells the story of walking into the plaster room one afternoon to unblock the sink. 'This little lad was yelling the place down. I couldn't see why. Anyway, the nurse in there pointed at me and whispered something to him. He went dead quiet. Then he said out loud, "It is him – Mr T from the A team." Well, I couldn't disappoint the lad. So when he asked me why my hair was longer than on TV, I said I'd got sick of it and decided to let it grow.' ■

Clive Anderson
Works Department

Clive Anderson is tall and good-looking, so it doesn't really come as a surprise that he was asked to meet the Princess of Wales. She had come to open a new building, and Clive was representing the Works Department on the day.

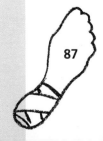

Ha Ha • Guffaw Guffaw • Tee H

Doctor, Doctor . . .

'Doctor, doctor, I'm having trouble with my breathing.'
'Well, I must give you something to stop that.'

'Doctor, doctor, we can't get into our house!'
'That's hardly my concern, is it?'
'Yes it is. The baby's swallowed the front-door key.'

'Doctor, doctor, I can't stop telling lies.'
'I don't believe you.'

'Doctor, doctor, everyone thinks I'm a cricket ball.'
'How's that?'
'Oh! – not you as well.'

'Doctor, doctor, I've only got fifty-nine seconds to live.'
'Wait a minute, please.'

'Doctor, doctor, I think I'm a pack of cards.'
'All right, I'll deal with you later.'

'Doctor, doctor, can you give me something for my liver?'
'How about a pound of onions?'

'Doctor, doctor, I think I've got measles!'
'That's a rash thing to say.'

'Doctor, doctor, what are you writing on my ankle?'
'Just a foot note.'

Doctor, doctor, I think I'm a goat.'
'How long have been like this?'
'Since I was a kid.'

'Doctor, doctor, I feel like a bell.'
'Take these pills and if they don't work give me a ring.'

'Doctor, doctor, I feel like an old sweater.'
'Well, I'll be darned.'

'Doctor, doctor, I keep feeling I'm invisible.'
'Who's that?'

Doctor, doctor, I feel like a racehorse!'
'Take these pills every four furlongs.'

'Doctor, doctor, I'm a burglar.'
'Have you taken anything for it?'

'Doctor, doctor, I keep thinking I'm a dog.'
'Sit down, please.'
'Oh, no – I'm not allowed on furniture.'

'Doctor, doctor, I think I'm shrinking.
'You'll just have to be a little patient.

Doctor, doctor my little sister thinks she's a lift.'
'Tell her to come in.'
'I can't, she doesn't stop at this floor.'

Chortle Chortle • Funny Ha Ha!

'Doctor, doctor, I think I've got flu.'
'OK, just stick your head out of the window, then poke your tongue out.'
'Will that make me better?'
'No, but I can't stand the man living opposite.'

'My doctor told me to give up golf.'
'Why – because of your health?'
'No. He looked at my scorecard.'

'This is a most unusual complaint, Mrs Thomas, have you had it before?'
'Yes, doctor.'
'Well, you've got it again.'

'Doctor, doctor, will these ointments clear up my spots?'
'I never make rash promises.'

'Doctor, doctor, I've just swallowed a roll of film.'
'Let's hope nothing develops.'

'Doctor, doctor, I'm boiling.'
'Just simmer down.'

'Doctor, doctor, can you help my daughter out?'
'Certainly, which way did she come in?'

'Doctor, doctor, I keep seeing double.'
'Sit on the couch, please.'
'Which one?'

'One of my aunts was a doctor but she gave it up.'
'Why?'
'She just didn't have the patients.'

'My uncle was a plastic surgeon until he sat on a radiator and melted.'

'Doctor, doctor, I've got the urge to paint myself gold all over.'
'Don't worry, you've just got a little gilt complex.'

'Well, now, is your cough better this morning?'
'It should be doctor, I've been practising all night.'

'Doctor, doctor, I think I'm a needle.'
'Yes, I see your point.'

A boy broke his arm playing football. After his arm had been put in plaster, he asked the doctor, 'When you take the plaster off, will I be able to play the violin?'
'Of course you will,' said the doctor.
'Great,' said the boy. 'I couldn't before you put it on.'

'I should never have taken my son to the ophthalmologist. He made a complete spectacle of himself.'

'Doctor, doctor, I think my goldfish is deaf.'
'He needs a herring aid.'

89

Profile • Profile •

Mr Bull performs all kinds of operation, from the routine – grommets, removing tonsils, pinning back ears – to more major and complicated procedures. An expert in laser surgery for laryngeal or throat conditions, such as benign tumours on the larynx and other problems that affect the voice, he is also a specialist in airway obstructions, particularly in tiny children whose tubes are very small.

He clearly enjoys ENT. 'It's a branch of surgery that covers all ages and a big range of operating from painstaking microsurgery to major head and neck cancer surgery.' He's never considered doing anything else: 'The good thing about ENT is you do usually get positive results.'

Just as well, as Mr Bull can operate on as many as six children on one of his regular afternoon theatre lists, and he can see up to sixty children in each morning clinic. So great is the number of children needing to be seen in Sheffield that Mr Bull has resorted to Saturday-morning clinics to reduce the waiting-lists.

He is scathing about the NHS reforms. 'Quite rightly, people should be made aware of the costs of what they're doing, but the money is not following the patients as the government promised. Departments like ours see little benefit from our increasing workload.' He gestures to the equipment surrounding him in the operating theatre.

Mr Bull
ENT Surgeon

'You know what I dislike about the Children's Hospital? The fag ends dumped outside the Casualty doors. If people didn't smoke, there'd be far fewer cancers of the larynx and children with breathing problems.' So muses Mr Bull, one of the Children's Hospital's more outspoken ear, nose and throat surgeons. He's been a consultant for fourteen years.

Profile • Profile

'Lots of this, like the lasers, bronchoscopes and TV monitors – all essential for the kind of surgery I do – don't even belong to the NHS. They've been bought with charity money.'

Mr Bull also teaches trainee surgeons. 'They keep me on my toes, these young enthusiasts, as they're up to the minute on the latest research and trends. Of course, they haven't got the experience . . .' He laughed cheerfully. Then, the phone rang to summon him to an emergency: a one-year-old baby with breathing problems on her way by ambulance. Just another day for Mr Bull. ■

Mr Bull and Abigail Oldfield, whose story is on the next page.

Ear, Nose and Throat Conditions

- Deafness, especially glue ear, a condition where fluid accumulates in the middle ear in the space behind the eardrum. Remedied by the insertion of grommets, small plastic tubes inserted into the eardrum which allow air into the middle ear and prevent the re-accumulation of fluid.

- Persistent ear infections requiring surgery on the bone in which the ear structures are embedded, or repair to perforated eardrums.

- Nasal conditions, such as obstruction or bleeding.

- Breathing difficulties due to obstruction of the upper air passages.

Some of the operations Mr Bull performs include:

- Operations to examine air passages, and on tonsils and adenoids.

- Specialised operations such as tracheotomies and laser surgery.

Children's Stories

Abigail in Hospital

Abigail came to the Children's Hospital to have an operation to pin back her ears.
When I went to the hospital, cameras were there. We had to walk in about nine
times. We went to a desk where a lady was and we asked her what we did next.
We went down a corridor into a room. A lady took us up to Ward 6 and gave us
a choice to go in a room, or in a room with other people. We chose a room
without people. Then we unpacked and they filmed us. Vicky came and asked us
some questions and they filmed that too. Vicky and Caroline were the nurses
who looked after me. We had a look round and found the play room. It didn't
have many toys that were grown up enough for me. So we came out and
unpacked a little bit. Later that night I had a bath in the hospital. Then they
filmed me coming out. Daddy and Ben came to see me and then we watched
television a bit and went to bed.

In the morning Caroline got me ready for my operation. I was worried about
it but I was looking forward to going on the trolly. I woke up on Saturday and I
felt sleepy. I had some breakfast and watched television. Nanan had sent me a
book and pencil to write with and I wrote a story called the Fairy's Land F. It was
about fairies and their statue of F which is like the Statue of Liberty only it is an F.
It is another world. A magical world. They woke up every morning and started to
fly about dusting the statue of F and then they all went to school and the
teachers went to teach and the mummys went and polished the floors in their
houses. Then they got the children's lunch ready and they delivered the lunches
to school.

I finished writing my story when the camera came to me again and I had to
pretend that I was just waking up. They took photographs of me. Then Daddy
and Ben came to take me home and Ben gave me a get well message. Then we
said good bye to the nurses and went home.   The End

Abigail Oldfield Age 7

Children's Stories

Short Stays

I had to get up very early and go to hospital to have some grommets put in. When I got to hospital me and my mum went to the desk and the nurse came to show me my bed and where the toilets were. She showed me the play room and the waiting room. We went back to the play room and played. Then the doctor came to talk to me and mum. When the doctor had gone a student nurse came to put some cream on my hand. Then she put a piece of plastic over them both and she took us to a place where there was a weighing scale. She told me to take my shoes off and stand on the weighing scale. Then she went to get somebody to come and check it. Then we went back to the play room and the student nurse took my temperature. Then we came to my bed and the doctor listened to my heart. Then a nurse came to tell me to get my night-dress on and my dressing-gown on. We went downstairs and I got on to the bed. When I woke up I was in the recovery room and a nurse gave me a glass of orange juice. Then she gave me a slice of toast. Then we had to wait for the doctor to come. When the doctor came he said you can go home.

Joanne Ellis Age 7

On Monday 9th of March I went in hospital to have four teeth out. I went on day case ward and the nice nurses let me watch a video. When it was time for my operation the nurse took my blood pressure and pulse, then they put a needle in the back of my hand and I went to sleep. When I woke up my teeth had gone and I was better.

Emma Grain Age 9

Drawings by Emma Grain, and Samantha Hiacliffe Age 7

93

Dr Mary Gerrard
Oncology Consultant

Dr Mary Gerrard is the Oncology Consultant at the Children's Hospital, and looks after all the children with malignant solid tumours on Ward 3. 'The great thing about working with children is that they can be seriously ill one moment, and then so much better the next. It can be terribly rewarding,' she says.

As a junior doctor, Mary Gerrard chose to specialise in oncology and has been at the Children's since 1988. 'People often ask me how I can do this, working all the time with children with cancer. I just feel that these are very ill children for whom I can really do something. What I do enjoy is that you can get to know the children and their families; you really feel you are part of their lives.'

Dr Gerrard emphasises how much the treatment of a child with cancer is a team effort. She works closely with the nurses and social workers on Ward 3, and takes a keen interest in whatever problems a child or family may be having because of the illness, be it returning to school, or needing emotional or practical support.

Dr Gerrard is also Secretary to the UK Children's Cancer Study Group, which carries out research. The majority of children with cancer are entered into nationwide UKCCSG trials, to compare different methods of treatment. 'The UKCCSG is a forum for all oncology specialists in this country to try and improve the treatment of tumours. We collect data on different kinds of cancer and swap notes on their treatment.' She says firmly, 'It's the only way we're going to make progress with this illness.' ■

Dr John Lilleyman waves at the wedding invitation sitting on his desk. 'That's what makes it all worthwhile. When years later one of my former leukaemia patients invites me to their wedding.' He smiles. 'That's what's changed since I started: the much bigger number of patients who survive and go on to live perfectly normal lives.'

So much so that Dr Lilleyman started up the Five Year Club, for children who have survived five years after the end of their treatment. At the first gathering back in 1977, there were just eight children. At the reunion party in 1987, there were over 140. The next will see those numbers doubled.

'I like it because its one of the few areas in medicine where looking after patients also ties in with working in the labs.' He not only treats children with leukaemia but also those with other blood disorders, such as haemophilia and life-threatening anaemias, who need regular transfusions.

But it's in the treatment of leukaemia that he has seen the biggest changes. 'It's much more labour intensive now: the children are given much more treatment. I still keep an eye on them as they get into their twenties, although some of the teenagers resent coming back to the Children's, especially if they still come with their mums! We just like to monitor how they are doing, and check that there's no recurrence of the disease. I once treated a little lad from Karachi – and I still get Christmas cards from the family!' ■

Dr John Lilleyman
Consultant Haematologist

Dr Lilleyman looks after all the children with leukaemia who come to the hospital. He has been the Consultant Haematologist at the Children's Hospital for eighteen years. Haematology is the study of the blood.

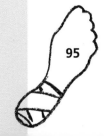

•Children's Stories•

Jonathan Laws' Story

Jonathan is sixteen months old. Looking at him now, it is hard to accept that he has had cancer. He is so full of life and so well. Yet only a few weeks ago we discovered he had a Wilms' tumour, a type of cancer of the kidney. I had found the tumour while changing him, although at the time I had no idea that the hard lump in his tummy could be anything as sinister as cancer.

Jonathan had to have many tests to determine the type and extent of the tumour. While he was injected, prodded and X-rayed, we waited anxiously for the results, trying to come to terms with this crisis in our lives. Being in the hospital helped tremendously. The staff were compassionate and understanding, and did much to soften the blow. Dr Gerrard in particular was so supportive, patiently answering our many questions.

Jonathan was lucky. The tumour had not spread and could be removed. It meant losing his kidney, but this seemed a small price to pay. We were assured that he could live normally with only one kidney, besides, the affected kidney was not functioning properly anyway.

He has just finished his chemotherapy with no adverse effects. His chances of survival are good and, despite the gruelling treatment his little body has gone through, he has bounced back quickly. In fact, he seems better than ever.

As for me, I'm still in one piece, although it will take some time before I recover completely, if that's possible. For now, I am confident Jonathan will make it and that's what keeps me going.

Cathy Laws (Mum)

Nursing revolves around the philosophy of 'family-centred care'. Louise explains, 'When parents are told that their child has a life-threatening disease, the news is devastating and they can feel they've lost control. Everything happens so quickly. We try to help them by involving all the family in all aspects of their child's care.'

Nurses also have a crucial role in providing support for the families. 'That's a big part of our job, just being here to talk to the parents and children. Explaining, teaching, listening and trying to dispel their fears and anxieties as they undergo their treatment. We just try to be someone that the families or the children can unburden themselves to.'

Nursing on Ward 3 is special. There are inevitably sad times when a child becomes very ill, or if treatment is unsuccessful. 'You do get very sad, you do have days when you just go home and cry,' says Louise, explaining how she copes. 'You feel a sense of loss and grief as the children become part of our lives for a time. But our loss is incomparable to that of the parents.'

Whilst recognising our own grief we have to be able to comfort the parents and relatives. One of the things that helps us all on Ward 3 is the strength, hope and humour that parents and children continually share with us.'

Louise King
Staff Nurse

'What I like about working on Ward 3', says Staff Nurse Louise King, 'is that you get to know the children and their families really well. They're here so much, sometimes for up to two years. You build up a really special relationship.' Louise has worked on Ward 3, the hospital's cancer ward, for over five years.

Children's Stories

Days of Confusion

Carla Spence, age 3, has leukaemia. Her mother writes:

22 December

Grandad, Mummy and Daddy have brought me to a place called a hospital. I don't like it, ladies called nurses keep sticking needles in me. I want to go home.

23 December

Mummy and Daddy showed me a book about leukaemia. They say it's something I've got. I hope it doesn't hurt like the needles do. I want to go home.

24 December

Santa's coming in his sleigh tonight. I hope he knows where to find me. I want to go home.

25 December

Santa did know where I was and now I've got lots of presents. I hate this place, I hate the nurses for hurting me. I hate Mummy for letting them. I want to go home.

26 December

Went to PACT house [see p.107] today for a while but it was nice to get back to hospital and see my friends. I like the nurses when they play with me. I love my Mummy but I still want to go home.

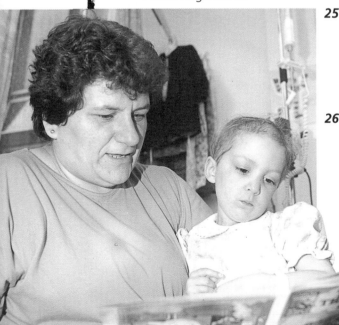

27 December

Needles, needles, and more needles, why do they keep sticking them in my hands, legs and back? Mummy make them stop, I hate you Mummy, take me home, please.

31 December

Nasty medicines and nasty pills, some to take home when Daddy and Grandad come to fetch me today. Mummy, could we please stay to paint just one more picture? I love you Mummy.

David Harwood's Story

I was at school in October 1991, when the headmaster brought me home from school. I had some bruises on my legs so my mum and dad had to bring me to Sheffield for some more blood tests (we had a lot of trouble finding the hospital). That afternoon I found out I had leukaemia and I had to stay in for a month. Which meant I did not have to go to school for a long time (thank goodness). Sometimes I get fed up of the injections and travelling to Sheffield. Everything was going well until November 92 when my leukaemia came back so now I am hoping that they will find me a ~~donor~~ bone marrow donor to make me well so I can get back to school. (Unfortunately).

David Harwood Age 11

Sadly, David died of his illness in May 1993. His parents asked that his story be included in his memory.

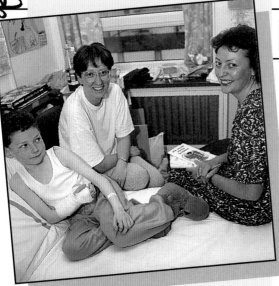

Jean Burrows
Social Worker

Jean Burrows (right) is a social worker at the hospital. Part of her job is to offer practical and emotional support to the families of patients being treated for cancer. This is her diary of a typical week.

Jean Burrows' Diary

Monday
The week begins at 8.30 with the morning's post. Typically, this includes vital cash grants for several families from the Malcolm Sargent Fund for Children with Cancer. I immediately forward a cheque for car repairs to one family, and another for new clothes to a single parent whose child has, as a side-effect of treatment, gained weight rapidly. At 9.30 I attend the ward round and learn about the admission of a new child with leukaemia.

A parent approaches me and asks if I can send a brief note to his employers to formally explain the reasons for his prolonged absence from work. We compose a letter and discuss the impact of their child's relapse on his wife and himself, and the stresses of caring for their other children.

In the afternoon I spend time with the mother of a gravely ill child on ICU. I'm revived in the afternoon by seeing at clinic a nine-year-old boy who completed treatment a year ago.

Tuesday
The day starts with a fortnightly meeting with Dr Gerrard, Sue Stephens – the Community Liaison Sister, Helen Vause – the Out-patient Clinic Sister, and Lesley Nicol – my fellow social worker. We discuss how to support several families caring for their terminally ill children at home.

At the afternoon clinic I see a ten-year-old girl and her mum, and chat with them about her recent return to school, three months after diagnosis. She received a sensitive and warm welcome and it's boosted her confidence considerably.

Wednesday

On Wednesdays I work as a member of the Child Sexual Abuse Treatment Team, offering counselling and play therapy to children and families where sexual abuse has occurred. Midway through the day I receive an unexpected phone call from a very distressed mum who falteringly tells me that her teenage son had died ten or fifteen minutes ago at home. His death was expected, but sudden and none the less heartbreaking. I arrange to visit the family tomorrow and phone Ward 3 to inform the staff and Dr Gerrard. We have known this lovely boy for over two years and we share in their enormous loss.

Thursday

First thing, I phone one of the hospital chaplains, Duncan Wilson, to ask him on the parents' behalf to make a contribution to the service of the youngster who died yesterday. My visit to his parents focuses on the events of the previous day and how they might best support and comfort their three other children. I leave them some story-books specially written for children to help them make sense of what is happening and the jumble of feelings they might have. I also check with them how the arrangements for the funeral service the following week are taking shape.

Friday

I spend an hour or so with the mum of a very young child recently diagnosed. Although growing more used to the ward and staff, both mother and child are still feeling frightened and uncertain. The mother is not sleeping very well on the ward Z-bed and is exhausted. I try to persuade her to snatch a nap during the day when her child is asleep. Her husband is unemployed and has a fifty-mile journey to the hospital to visit them, and inevitably the travelling expenses are eating a large hole in his pocket. I telephone an urgent request to the Malcolm Sargent Fund to cover the cost of his initial fifteen train journeys. ∎

Drawing by Darren Redmond

That's my dad, he said he wishes he was me, I don't know why!

Solid Tumours

- Cancer is rare in childhood but can occur at any age. It is usually quite different from that seen in adults.

- It occurs in different tissues in the body, for example, kidney, brain, lymph glands or bones. Symptoms differ, depending on the site of the disease.

- Many cancers are revealed by the presence of a lump, usually referred to as a tumour. Not all lumps are malignant cancers; some tumours are benign, and some lumps may not be tumours at all.

- The majority of children with cancer can be cured with intensive and often prolonged courses of treatment.

- Chemotherapy – the treatment of cancer by drugs – is the most commonly used type of treatment. Sometimes surgery and radiotherapy are also necessary.

- The treatment intended to destroy the cancer cells is chosen after tests which determine exactly what type of cancer it is, exactly where it is, and whether it has spread from the original site.

Ward 3 is the region's specialist centre for the treatment of children with cancer.

7.30 a.m. The ward is hushed, curtains still drawn round the beds. Bunty's mum emerges from a cubicle. Staff Nurse Louise King, arriving for her day shift, waves cheerfully before disappearing into the Nurses Office for the morning report.

8.15 a.m. Charge Nurse Alan Beddows, who runs the ward, frowns. It's a Wednesday, clinic day and busy: the ward is already nearly full. In addition, one of his staff nurses is off sick, so the ward will be short-staffed.

9 a.m. Children are sitting on their beds eating Ricicles. Luke, aged four, is already running up and down the corridor with gleeful cries. The curtains remain pulled round Bunty's bed. She's having a much-needed lie in.

9.30 a.m. Competing for attention with the *Home Alone* video on the televisions, Dr Mary Gerrard, the consultant, begins her ward round.

10.30 a.m. Wednesday is Baking Day and three-year-old Carla Spence is helping Lorraine, the ward teacher, to make rock cakes before she goes down to Theatre for a lumbar puncture. Charge Nurse Alan is checking to see who is due to go home today. He has a new admission and there's no spare bed . . .

11.30 a.m. A trolley returns from Theatre with a drowsy Carla Spence. Louise is busy in the treatment room, where she's been all morning helping Rachel, the junior doctor, give chemotherapy.

12 noon Lunch, meat and potato pie, arrives. Karen, the nursery nurse, serves it up to children engrossed in Lego and jigsaws. Louise, still busy in the treatment room, wonders whether she'll have time for a sandwich.

1.30 p.m. Carla has perked up and wants a rock cake. It's Luke's turn for his injection. There are loud screams, and seconds later, Luke emerges sporting a Ninja Turtles sticky plaster. 'I had a needle,' he says proudly, 'and I screamed.' As Luke and his family set off home, Alan is pleased to have solved the beds problem and Rachel can admit the new patient.

3.30 p.m. Karen and Carla paint clowns' faces, while Bunty decorates a birthday card with sequins. Louise, tired at the end of a long day, slips out of the door as Tracey Shinwell, the ward assistant, hops through on crutches, her leg in plaster. 'I've broken my knee,' she says ruefully. 'That's me off for four weeks.' Alan rolls his eyes.

5.30 p.m. Children's tea arrives: baked potatoes and beans. There's a special request for ice cream, and it's brought from the hospital kitchens. *Neighbours* echoes round the ward.

7.30 p.m. The ward is dark, with pools of light above a few beds. Mums unfold Z-beds. Carla's mother quietly reads her a story. Once again silence reigns.

Leukaemia

● The majority of children with cancer can now be cured, and it has been estimated that by the year 2000, around 1 person in 1000 will be a survivor of childhood cancer.

● Leukaemia is a cancer of the bone marrow and is the commonest malignant growth in childhood.

● It is still a rare disease, and the chances of developing it during the first fourteen years of life are less than 1 in 1000.

● Its cause is unknown.

● There are several different types of leukaemia, of which the large majority are acute lymphoblastic leukaemia (ALL) and the minority are acute myeloblastic leukaemia (AML).

● Most children recover from leukaemia but the road to recovery is long and hard, involving injections and spells of time in hospital. The full schedules run from six months to two years, and even when treatment has finished a close eye is kept on children for three to four years to check for signs of recurrence.

Our Work is Play: The Nursery Nurses

The most dramatic difference between a children's hospital and the adult equivalent is this: a children's hospital is a lot more fun.

It is partly to do with the colourful clowns and pictures on the walls, partly the bite-size tables and chairs. Most of all, it is down to the nursery nurses.

They use play to help alleviate stress and fear, the emotions you naturally associate with being hospitalised. Encouraging a child to draw a picture of an operation before the event or paint one after it is an excellent way to help deal with the anxiety he or she may be feeling. Some children find it difficult to express their fears verbally. Playing with dolls, toy syringes and masks can help bring out a whole range of questions, worries or misconceptions.

Gill Kelly, one of the two nursery nurses in Accident and Emergency, tells the story of a little girl who used to scream every time she went into the anaesthetic room. 'Nobody knew why. But it came out in play that she hated the smell. Once we knew what it was, we could do something about it and she never screamed again.'

Adult hospitals take note – if you want your patients better prepared for operations, less anxious, and recovering quicker, you could do far worse than employ a team of nursery nurses.

In the following poem, Nursery Nurse Clair Barker sums up how she sees her work . . .

The Nursery Nurse

In winter, in summer, in autumn and spring,
In a green skirt or trousers and T-shirt-type thing,
We're here on the wards all over the place
Putting a smile on each child's face.

'Who is it?' you ask, with the paint in her hair,
The glue on her shoe and a look of despair
As she looks in the playroom to see the melée –
It's the Nursery Nurse, the bringer of play.

With scissors and paper, some junk and white glue
You'll be quite amazed at what you can do:
Birthday cards, models, we'll help you to make,
Keeping you busy the hours you're awake.

We paint on the windows, on walls
we display
The pictures and posters you've made
through the day.
Games are our favourites, like Trivial Pursuit
(I won twice last week when I played
Michael Shoot).

Procedures and questions to you
we'll explain
Preparing for theatre, halves all your pain.
Our ears are for listening to all of
your woes –
'Will it hurt?' 'Will I ever again see my toes?'

We relieve all the pressure, alleviate stress,
Annoying the doctors by making a mess
With glitter and sand and playdough
of lime (Which sticks to the floor for a very
long time!).

We don't mind your music, your chatter
and noise,
We're all well aware of today's girls
and boys.
From Turtles to Segas and sports
cars electric
You can play what you like, be it quiet
or hectic.

From one to sixteen, we've got something
for you,
Or bring your own toys, it's all up to you.

But remember us most when you're home
again, well,
Your illness all cured by potions that smell.
We're still painting pictures on windows
and doors
And the playdough we used is still stuck on
the floors.

Children's Stories

Bunty's Story

Bunty Purkayastha, aged thirteen, came into the Children's with pains in her chest in September 1992. After X-rays, ultrasound and scans, she had an operation – a biopsy – on her back.

October   After my operation, I found myself in ICU. Then I was moved on to Ward 3. I felt very confused and angry because I was very poorly and didn't understand why I had been moved. I thought that the doctors were meant to make me better, but I was worse than before I came in. Then Dr Gerrard explained to me that I had a tumour on my right lung, which would eventually need operating on again. I didn't trust her very much at first. To make matters worse, a week later I started chemotherapy. This gave me mouth ulcers and the nurses had to fight with me to take my mouth ulcer medicine, so I didn't like the nurses very much either. I had to have a thumb prick each day. This was to check my blood count. Most of the time, it was low, that's why I was so tired.

November   In November, I was allowed to go home to stay for two days. I enjoyed it very much and didn't want to go back to hospital, but I had to.

I then went home again the day before my birthday. It was my thirteenth birthday, it was the best birthday I'd ever had. All my school friends came to visit me, and all my primary school friends came, and my neighbours.

Near the end of November I had a scan. Dr Gerrard and some surgeons looked at my scan. Then they told my mum and dad that they would be able to remove most of the tumour by surgery.

December   On the 2nd of December, I had the operation. I now only stay in hospital every three weeks for chemo and come for a check-up each week. Other than that, I'm at home with my tutor, or at school.

Profile • Profile

The signal is given and with a cheer one thousand balloons fly swiftly away into the blue spring sky. It's the PACT balloon race. Sheila Jackson, the PACT Co-ordinator smiles. Another successful event and another £1000 raised for PACT.

PACT makes an essential contribution to the hospital's Cancer Centre. It provides funding for research and has bought equipment for Ward 3 and a special microscope for Dr Lilleyman.

But PACT is also about providing fun, and runs a lively social calendar for the children. It has also bought a large house near the hospital where families can stay to be nearer their children on Ward 3.

Money is raised in many ways and the driving force behind it all is Sheila Jackson. She became involved when her daughter Rachel was diagnosed with leukaemia at the age of six. After she died, Sheila took on the job of running PACT. 'This place was so good to Rachel and me, nurses and everybody. They couldn't have cared more. I just wanted to try and give something back.'

Sheila always provides an understanding shoulder to cry on. 'I feel, because of what happened to Rachel, that I really can offer more. Being told your child has cancer is the worst thing in the world. Well, I've faced the worst and I can understand what parents are going through in a way the doctors and the nurses perhaps can't,' she says.

'I just want to feel that when the children come in here, they really are going to get the best of everything.' ∎

PACT

PACT, the Parents Association for Children with Tumours and Leukaemias, is a registered charity at the Children's Hospital. It raises funding for research and for providing support for children with cancer and their families.

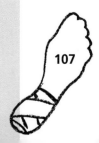

Penny Piece: How the Labs Play their Part

Dr Mary Gerrard spoke quietly to Mrs Edwards about Lesley. She had not liked the look of that lump, so Haematology did some blood tests to check on the number of red cells and white cells, and someone looked at a thin film of the blood on a microscope slide. Chemical Pathology also checked the blood for the levels of life's essential common chemicals, and a urine sample for anything unusual. Lesley had to go to Theatre for Miss Jenny Walker to remove the lump, so Haematology checked that any bleeding would stop naturally, and a pint of blood was 'cross matched' in case Lesley needed it. The lump was in a capsule or shell and came out quite easily. It was sent to Histopathology where it was dissected and pieces of it cut thin enough for the pathologists to see its cells and structure through a microscope. They told Mary that it had been a tumour which Lesley was born with; that Jenny had taken all of the lump out; and that there was no sign of it anywhere else. Follow-up by further tests in Haematology and Chemical Pathology had shown that Lesley was now just like other children, and Mr and Mrs Edwards would soon be taking her home.

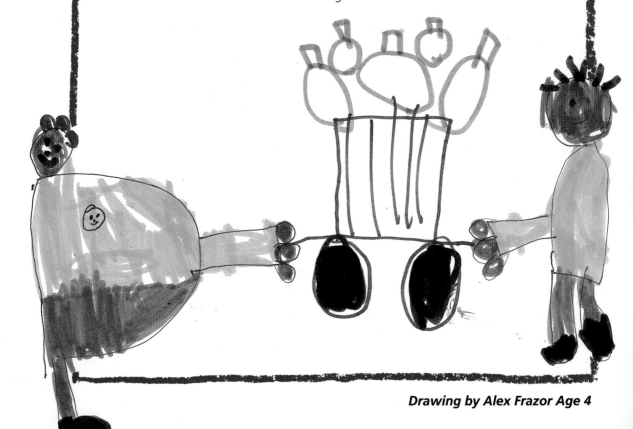

Drawing by Alex Frazor Age 4

Children's Stories

A Day on Ward 3

Time	Story	
(clock)	Time to get up and washed. Bleep, Bleep! First drug change today.	(illustration)
(clock)	This breakfast looks nice. Its mine so keep your mits off!!	(illustration)
(clock)	Doctors came round to see how I was. Bedpan time!	(illustration)
(clock)	Dinner time. This looks alright. It tastes quite nice as well. Bedpan time! Where's Nurse Ivy!	(illustration)
(clock)	Hospital radio man came round I had 'Why can't I wake up with you' by Take-That.	(illustration)
(clock)	Its tea time this I thought was nice. It even looks nice. Bedpan time again!!	(illustration)
(clock)	I had some visitors who played some games with me. They bring me chocolates and grapes	(illustration)
(clock)	Get undressed and mum and dad try and settle me down for the night.	(illustration)
(clock)	Time for the big Hydration bag and anti-sickness tablet.	(illustration)

By Anna Coulton Age 11

Profile • Profile

Dr Mike Smith
Consultant Paediatrician

Mike Smith was a junior doctor when he first saw how some doctors broke bad news. A woman had recently given birth to her first son. The consultant said to her, 'Do you know he's got Down's? Do you know what that is?'
'No, er . . .'
'He's a mongol. He'll never be able to knock the top off an egg. Anything else you wanted to know? No? Good.'

Luckily, things have changed in the NHS. Now himself a consultant, running the Ryegate Assessment Centre with Dr Chris Ritty, Mike Smith's approach is very different. His patients are children who, for a variety of reasons, have learning difficulties.

To an outsider his job seems among the most difficult in the hospital. Children with cerebral palsy or Down's do not 'get better'. There's no magic drug to spirit the diseases away, and much of his energy and skill goes into supporting the families.

'My aim is for parents to get a real understanding of the child's difficulty. To try to encourage a completely different set of expectations.' This can be a slow process. It takes hours of conversation over a long period. Parents have to start from scratch, building a very different idea of who their child is. He wants to give them back a sense of power and purpose that at first the condition takes away.

'It gives me satisfaction if parents know how to make the best use of the services available – if they know where they are going and what they want to achieve.' At Ryegate they put parents in touch with local support groups and other parents. It is hard to overestimate how much families value feeling they are not on their own.

'There's a limit to what we can do medically. But the therapists here – occupational, physio, communication – make a tremendous difference to a child's quality of life. That's what counts.' ∎

Ian Whitehead's Story

Anne Whitehead has got to know Ryegate very well over the last few years. Ian, her son, was born profoundly brain-damaged in 1983.

I spent Easter 1993 with my son Ian at the Children's Hospital. He was being treated for pneumonia in the Intensive Care Unit, and I had to make crucial decisions about his life.

I dearly love my son – a much wanted child. At his birth, my husband and I were immediately faced with the decision as to whether he should be ventilated, and we feared for his life. He survived, and the following two years became a time of great uncertainty and emotional upheaval. We became aware of the enormity of Ian's disabilities and how they would affect our lives. It is difficult for parents facing their child's handicap to believe that life can ever be good again. I was in the fortunate position of having a strong marriage, loving support from my friends and family, and the ability to find the professional help we needed for Ian's potential to be realised. Life did prove to be good again because we did everything in our power to make Ian's life worthwhile.

Nobody would choose this for themselves but in painfully working through all the problems I have found strengths and resources inside me, and I have grown as a person. The natural panic and anxiety which all mothers feel when their child is at risk have to be repressed in order to deal with the immediate problem. But all the repressed feelings have to be dealt with at some stage and I am still learning how to handle these. This is more difficult because I no longer have the emotional support of my husband who died two years ago.

Easter 1993 was a very difficult time for me. Ian was in a critical condition and I was being asked to face the same dilemma as when he was born. This time I was absolutely convinced I didn't want to lose this lovely child who I had grown so close to over his nine years. He has brought so much to my life and I love him for that.

Ian came home on April 27th fully recovered. We've come through another crisis which has drawn us even closer together.

Jane Smith
Physiotherapist

The children Jane Smith works with cannot be cured by a quick operation or a course of drugs. She is a physiotherapist at Ryegate Children's Centre, and sees children experiencing difficulties in development. For fifteen years she has been part of a team of doctors, speech therapists, occupational therapists and others who assess and support children with conditions like cerebral palsy and muscular dystrophy, and premature babies born with brain damage.

Profile • Profile •

As Jane assesses a child at play she's looking at a whole variety of indicators: muscle tone, joint ranges, how the child moves and whether the movements are fluid. Jane asks herself, 'Is the child at a level appropriate to his or her age?' If not, Jane wants to know why. Inevitably, enormous parental anxiety surrounds a child's assessment. 'Some come here and leave very relieved because, deep down, they've known something was wrong, and now someone's going to do something about it. Others are full of disbelief and anger.'

For children she sees long term, 'It's almost like becoming part of the family.' Having two children of her own, Jane admits, made her more realistic about the demands she makes on parents: 'Just getting to an appointment can be hell.'

'Will my child walk?' is one of the most difficult questions Jane is asked. 'I never say yes if I'm not certain. It's unfair to raise hopes.' She aims to encourage parents to understand what's going wrong and become their own physiotherapists. They are with the child all the time: 'For these children physiotherapy isn't half an hour of exercise. It's everything – how they eat, sit and sleep.'

• Profile • Profile

*Reading a book while standing up:
physiotherapy takes all forms.*

The difficulties facing the children and families at Ryegate can sound overwhelming to outsiders, but Jane and her colleagues remain happy and optimistic.

'The joy is seeing any amount of progress. A simple smile can be a huge reward.' ■

Down's Syndrome

Down's syndrome is a condition where the child has an abnormal number of chromosomes.

● The number of cases is about 1 in 600–800 births.

● The child has facial and body characteristics which are recognisable as Down's syndrome: small facial features with slightly upslanting eyes, small round ears, sometimes a cardiac defect such as a hole in the heart, unusual patterns of crease development in the hands and feet.

● Sometimes the bowel can be obstructed and the children are floppy.

● Children with Down's syndrome have a higher than average incidence of hearing impairment and occasional visual difficulties.

● Additional medical complications include underactivity in the thyroid gland.

● The condition is lifelong and is almost always associated with severe learning retardation.

● It is important to recognise these children at birth and support their families from the moment of diagnosis.

Cerebral Palsy

- The condition is acquired in early life. It is lifelong but does not get worse.
- Most cases are determined very early in the pregnancy and rarely are they due to abnormalities in the process of birth.
- The number of cases is about 1 in 500 births.
- Damage (or malformation) in a small part of the brain means that messages don't get through to the arms and legs.
- Occasionally it affects other areas of the body.

There are three types of cerebral palsy:

- *The spastic type* can affect the legs only (diplegia), all of the body, or just one side of the body (spastic hemiplegia). Therapy aims to improve the condition by breaking down spasticity as much as possible. Education about posture and movement for both the child and the parents is important.

- In *athetoid cerebral palsy* the child has difficulty in co-ordinating movement, and when reaching for an object makes many extraneous and unhelpful movements. This type of cerebral palsy is very difficult to treat and requires physical training (physiotherapy) and attention to correct posture and seating.

- With *ataxic cerebral palsy*, a child has wobbly movement and very often low muscle tone. This is the least common form of the disease.

Stephen Mower Age 8

Profile • Profile

'I 've got to squeeze eight hundred staff, all the toddlers' parents and any contractors into eighty spaces in three car parks. And there's only one of me. I like to see the job as a challenge.'

In earlier days he's worked as a butcher, a car body repairer, and a warehouseman in a huge freezer store – which is probably the best training for being out in all weathers. In really bad conditions he's covered from head to foot in oilskins and a yellow sou'wester. But there is little protection from some irate folk who won't accept that the car park is full.

'I'm the first point of contact in the hospital. Parents come here anxious and worried about their nipper. If there are just no spaces, sometimes I'm the one they take it out on. I've even had one dad throw a bottle at me. But that kind of behaviour just strengthens my resolve.' Michael is 5 feet ¼ inch tall.

He knows people by their cars. 'I've got the occasional nickname for my best regular customers. One mum had a large car I'd just found the last – very small – space for. It wasn't going to be easy. Well, she just drove straight in. One manoeuvre. I couldn't believe it. From that day on, she's been Mrs Mansell.'

Michael's always got time for a chat. Many long-stay parents comment that his smile and jokes help to keep them going at a tough time. ■

Michael Ryan
Car Park Attendant

Michael Ryan holds down one of the toughest jobs in the hospital. Some mums and dads see him as an obstacle, others as a friend. But whether you're a paediatrician, a parent or a patient, you can't avoid him.

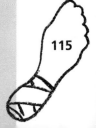

115

All in a Day: Day Care

For most children a trip to Ward 8, the Day Care Ward, is more like a day out than a day in hospital. The staff work hard to keep it like that. Lots of colour on the walls, a playroom full of toys, a family room complete with sofas, goldfish bowl and TV all help to create a feeling of home from home. And a nurse has usually shown the family round on an earlier visit to give them an idea of what to expect.

Up to twelve children in the morning and the same number in the afternoon arrive every day. They come for special tests, investigations or minor operations, all of which can be done quickly. The advantage to the child and a mum and dad is clear: only half a day or so off work, less time away from home, no overnight stays in unfamiliar surroundings. In short, the least disruption to family life.

Cynics may pipe up, 'The hospital is saving money by only keeping them in for a day,' but the point is that studies have shown that the less you disrupt a child's life, the more easily he or she can cope with the disruption and the quicker the child heals. Of course, day care is only appropriate for those procedures that need no more than a few hours' recuperation.

Fun is the theme. If the child is happy, the trip to Theatre can be on a miniature motorised police bike or car. Most children jump at the chance and, providing there has been no 'pre-med', there are not many cases of driving under the influence! Care continues for a couple of hours after Theatre. Some sleep, then a light snack (if it's wanted) and off home. The following day a district nurse visits to check that all is well.

Rachel Griffiths, age 5, in bed on
Day Care
Opposite are the staff on Day Care

Day Care's Top Ten Procedures

- Ear, nose and throat operations
- Reduction of fractured noses
- Removal of foreign bodies
- Circumcision for religious or medical reasons
- Hernia repairs
- Urodynamics (investigations into bladder functions)
- Correction of curly toes
- Dental extractions
- Change of plaster of Paris
- Plastic surgery (removal of birth marks and moles)

•Children's Stories•

In and Out in a Day

First the doctor came to see us. He told me about the cream he was going to put on my hands. He said, 'First we will put some cream on your hands and then we will put a needle in you to make you sleep. Then I just sat on my bed watching the children play. They all seem to be enjoying themselves to say they are in the hospital. When I was here I helped a little girl with the Sega as I know a bit about it. The sister has just been to put me my cream on. It feels very funny. She was very nice and pleasant. And so are all the other staff. The doctor came to see me as well to take my details. I am the last to go down as I am the oldest and the rest are younger than me.

I have now had my operation and I am sitting up having a drink not feeling too well. I am waiting to be discharged now but I must say my short stay in the Children's Hospital was a very nice one. When I grow up I would like to do some of the nice work they do looking after people. Just like they did me and all the other children.

That's the end now.
All I must say is a big thankyou.

Sarah Jackson Age 11

My Visit to Daycare
I have come to have a lump took out of my face.
I will have a little operation on this. My nurse
came. Her name was Ann. She asked me
questions about myself.

Holly Brodie Age 8

Drawing by Victoria Heinstiffe Age 9

Rehman and Arfan Mohammed and Shabana Kosser are brothers and sister who come in every month for a blood transfusion.

This is me and my two brothers on Daycare to have our transfusions every month. While I am here I play with the computer or I play with the dolls then we go home at 6 o'clock. We do sticking on Daycare.

Shabana Kosser Age 9

This is me in my bed on the Daycare Ward. I come to Daycare every month for a blood transfusion. While I am here I play on the computer and then I go home at 6 o'clock.   The end

Rehman Mohammed Age 8

Thalassaemia

Rehman Mohammed and his brother and sister have Thalassaemia.
Thalassaemia is a hereditary blood disorder most common around the Mediterranean, in the Middle East, South-East Asia and Africa.
There are three types: major, intermediate and minor.
If a child has a major type they require regular blood transfusions, without which life expectancy is only a few years.
If the disorder goes untreated the children get severe anaemia, thin bones and fractures.

Drawings by Shabana Kosser

Sylvia Worsman

**Tucked away at the back of the hospital is a small building that houses the chapel and mortuary.
If you never get to know it exists, the hospital are more than happy. For the vast majority of parents that's the way it is. But for a very few it cannot be so.**

The chapel and mortuary are meant to be physically on the fringe of the hospital, but the woman who looks after them is at the very heart of life at SCH.

Sylvia Worsman came to the hospital over twenty years ago, as a mortuary technician. In that time she has given a fund of warmth and love to the parents whose children have not recovered from serious illness, and in particular to those parents who have suffered a cot death. Consultants, nurses, doctors and lab technicians alike all acknowledge that, without Sylvia, the hospital's support for families in their bleakest of times would just not be the same.

'It never gets any easier. Every time I go to see a family who've lost a little one my mouth's dry, my heart's beating, I'm tense. Of course, it's nothing compared with what they must be going through. I try and treat them the way I'd like to be treated if I were in their position. Give them love, and listen and assure them their child is going to get the same care and attention with me as they've had on the ward. Nothing is too good for their child. Some of them have had such short lives.'

Sylvia feels strongly that for many of us death is so powerful a taboo we'd rather hide it, if not forget about it altogether. When she started to run the department, she threw away all the shrouds. Her mortuary is practically alone in the country in having sheets, blankets and pillows. Modest about the strength she has given grieving families, Sylvia would be the last person to let tell that in 1988 she received the British Empire Medal for her work.

One other activity (which could not be more different from her professional work) puts Sylvia in touch with dozens of parents and visitors. Sylvia sells in the region of fifty sweatshirts and T-shirts a month, emblazoned with the SCH logo. For most people her time raising money for the hospital's League of Friends would be a nine-to-five job. 'Some people say I've missed my vocation,' she says. If times are ever particularly hard in the NHS, she knows there's a budding career waiting in Sheffield's Meadowhall (the largest covered shopping centre in Europe).

If she's not taking a size medium in blue to a sister on Ward 3, then Sylvia's busy planning the Spring or Summer Fayre or one of several jumble sales to raise money for the hospital. Does she sit on the committee of the League of Friends? 'No,' she says, starting to laugh. 'Floorcloth, that's me! Just here to help.'

That would be the last word anyone at Sheffield Children's Hospital would use to describe Sylvia Worsman. ■

Drawing by Stephen Mower Age 8

121

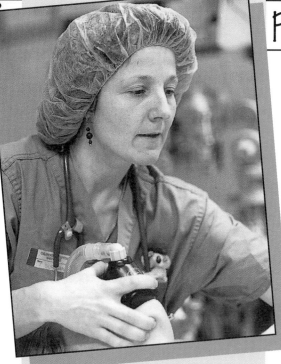

Dr Teresa Dorman
Consultant Anaesthetist

As one of the hospital's consultant anaesthetists, Teresa Dorman is responsible for her patients at a critical time. She puts them to sleep for theatre, monitors them during the operation and, of course, brings them round.

It's the moment every mother dreads. You're carrying your child down the hospital corridor. All he's wearing is a gown. Past Theatre reception, through two sets of double doors, and then into a clinically sterile room. There's a blur of monitors and instruments. A team of nurses and doctors all in green is waiting. You've got to hand him over. They're smiling but you're not sure why. They lay him down on a trolley, head close to two or three cylinders of gas. The ward nurse leaves. A doctor starts whispering reassuring words in your child's ear. Tears are welling up and you're trying to hold them back. Then the doctor looks up: 'Thanks, Mum, you've done really well. Thanks.' A nurse ushers you away. To wait.

It's a moment of dread no parent wants to experience more than once in a lifetime. On average, Teresa Dorman goes through it twenty times a week – not counting emergencies. As a consultant anaesthetist at SCH, part of her job is to take as much dread out of the anaesthetic as possible. Staff on the ward will use story-books to explain the process to the child. Teresa visits the parents the night before the operation, makes sure they understand what's going to happen and then monitors the child constantly from the moment she's put him to sleep until the moment she brings him round.

'The sight of your child being made unconscious so suddenly is enough to upset anyone. Some mums and dads are better than others. Generally, dads are better than mums. Men hide their feelings more than women. And tears – from mum or dad – are enough to set off a child, sometimes panic them.'

The job has its extremes: a toddler can be sitting happily on his mum's knee listening to her read from *Peter Pan*, blissfully unaware that Teresa's given him a waft of 'magic wind', or gas, then a waft or two more. The mask goes on. Mum stops reading. It's been relatively painless. On the other hand, a five-year-old can be screaming and crying: 'There's no point in trying reason then, they're beyond reason. They're in no state for an injection. So I turn the gas up and they take in huge lungfuls because they're so upset. Sounds tough. But it's the quickest way to get them to sleep.'

Generally an anaesthetic injection is pretty much instantaneous. But in the case of a child who's upset or whose hands are very cold and veins apparently non-existent, gas is better. Sometimes Teresa uses a combination: an injection to put the child to sleep, then, just as that is beginning to wear off, gas to keep them asleep. It's a careful balancing act. She's checking all the time to ensure the child isn't 'light' – that is to say, isn't coming out of the anaesthetic. The tell-tale signs are rising heartbeat and blood pressure, enlarged pupils, hands starting to sweat – the signs of the 'fight and flight' mechanism we all have when our bodies are stressed. ■

More About Anaesthetics

In more complex operations, Teresa gives a cocktail of drugs: a form of opiate to suppress the senses and the pain, a paralysing agent to relax the muscles, and the anaesthetic gas to 'numb' the brain. Here the balancing act is more complicated and demands more skill, and the child can take far longer to come round – anything up to thirty minutes. If it's a premature baby who's not well before the anaesthetic, then constant monitoring is even more critical – they can fall very ill very quickly.

Once the critical task of bringing the child round has been completed, pain control is the next job of the anaesthetist. If a small baby has had major bowel surgery or a lass has had a frame put on her foot to lengthen it, then Teresa would continue using morphine after the operation as well. Some children might need it for two or three days, some babies longer.

Jan Rooney
Recovery Sister

'We're the nurses that get no cards and no chocolates,' jokes Sister Jan Rooney. Since 1977, when she began work in Recovery at the hospital, she can only recall receiving ten boxes of chocolates. 'Nobody knows we're here,' she says wistfully. Recovery is a small but crucial part of the hospital, the staging post between the operating theatre and the ward. Here children spend a relatively short but anxious time after their operations, coming round from the general anaesthetic.

In 1992, 4115 children passed safely through the hands of Sister Rooney and her colleagues in Recovery, where children can spend anything from five minutes to an hour or two. Sister Rooney herself has been here for fourteen-and-a-half years.

In Recovery the television is always on: 'You'd be amazed how many children come round saying, "Is that *Neighbours*?"' If appropriate, parents are invited down to see their children in Recovery. Very few hospitals encourage this, but for Sister Rooney it is all part of reminding children that the operation is over. Parents sometimes worry when she tells them it will be two hours before they can see their child, when the surgeon has told them that the tonsil operation will only last twenty minutes. 'It's recovery from the anaesthetic which takes the time.'

Although most children pass straight through, there can be anxious moments as the nurses monitor breathing, heart rate and blood pressure. 'We're looking for any deviation from the normal reversal of anaesthesia.' She still finds it hard to predict how any child will respond. 'Some have a major operation and come straight round. Others have a simple op and take ages.'

Sister Rooney does not take kindly to Recovery being referred to as a production line. 'We try very, very hard to give a personal service.'

But what about the shortage of chocolates? 'Our treat is seeing the children get better and go out of those doors.' ■

A Touch of Radio Therapy:
Chrystal Radio and TV

'**C**hrystal Radio.' The jingle buzzes out of the speaker and drowns the sound of the cleaner mopping the floors in the otherwise empty corridor. It's evening: clinics are over, children are eating tea on their beds and the hospital's very own radio station is jumping into life through a jungle of loudspeakers on every ward.

Tucked away in a suite of cupboards on the third floor above the junior doctors' mess is a mega media empire. From 5 p.m. every day, a host of volunteers creep into the hospital and for a few hours the airwaves are humming with the latest from Take That or Postman Pat. Founded ten years ago by volunteer Laurence Newman, Chrystal Radio has recently been refurbished, so now parents and children alike can ring in direct with their requests.

'I hope we provide a service that really cheers up the children,' says Laurence.

Every day the volunteers, budding young DJs, visit the wards to ask children for their requests. Funded entirely by charity donations, they've built up an impressive collection of records. 'We can usually play whatever the children want. We've got a full range from pop hits to younger children's songs and music,' says Matt, aged sixteen, and the DJ on Wednesday nights.

Chrystal Television was set up just eighteen months ago and puts together afternoons of programmes presented from its very own extra-small broom cupboard! Every week the nurses and doctors nominate a 'Patient of the Week', and the Chrystal team go and film their own special message on the ward!

Cartoons by Gillian Longbottom Age 14

•Children's Stories•

Chrystal Radio

My name is Gillian, and I have a friend, Carole, who is a Ward 5 nurse. We took an exciting trip one evening to the Chrystal Radio studio! Although the studio is tiny, there was some pretty high-tech stuff around. We were shown how everything works, far too technical for me, and there's no use asking Carole!!

I was introduced on the radio by this very good looking fella, who wants to work on Children's TV!! If Andy Peters can do it – well! We think he'll walk it.

We were asked a few questions and then they insisted I announced my surname – Longbottom. Revenge will be mine one day, especially on Carole!

I was given the chance to play my favourite record, 'Oh! Carolina' (not 'Oh! Carole') by Shaggy. The DJ said he was sick of it but, because it was for me, he would allow it. I then read a silly story, it was embarrassing. We had a super time and eventually said goodbye, leaving with stars in our eyes. Fame, fortune, men, big ears, all after ten minutes 'on the air' – I could get used to this, and thanks for cheering my day up.

Profile • Profile

It's 7.30 a.m. and Joy Cookson is sorting a mountain of post into pigeon-holes. 'What I love about this job,' she says cheerfully, 'is meeting people.' As the hospital's post lady, Joy knows *everybody*. She believes in personal service and hand-delivers mail twice a day to every department in the hospital.

Joy has worked at the hospital for nineteen years. She started out by delivering sterile gauzes and cotton wool to the wards, but now runs the postal service from a small room in the basement. She sorts out hundreds of letters each day, and franks all the hospital's outgoing mail. ■

Joy Cookson
The Postwoman

Pam Rawding and Diane Lazenby
The Switchboard

Tucked away in a cubicle near A & E lives the switchboard. Twenty-four hours a day, the women who work here put parents in touch with the wards and keep hospital staff in touch with the world. This is the nerve centre of the hospital: only 'switch' keep a track of the comings and goings of hospital staff: they field 362 616 incoming calls a year, 1007 a day.

On the wall are the boxes for sixty short-range bleepers for use within the hospital, and fifty-three long-range pagers with a ten-mile radius for staff on call at home. And there are the 'crash' or emergency bleepers, for fire or cardiac arrests.

Of course, not all doctors stay close to their bleepers, but, in the end, no doctor can hide from switch for long. ■

• Thank-you •

I would like to say a BIG
thank you to All the Doctors and
nurses who helped make me well
again.

thankyou

thank you

thank you

OXYGEN